THE IGNATIAN TRADITION

SPIRITUALITY IN HISTORY SERIES

The Ignatian Tradition

Kevin F. Burke, s.j.

Eileen Burke-Sullivan

Phyllis Zagano, Series Editor

LITURGICAL PRESS
Collegeville, Minnesota

www.litpress.org

Cover design by Ann Blattner. *Saint Ignatius Writing the Constitutions* by Jusepe de Ribera (1565–1652). Used with permission from The Institute of Jesuit Sources, Saint Louis, Missouri.

2	3	4	5	6	7	8	9

Library of Congress Cataloging-in-Publication Data

The Ignatian tradition / Kevin F. Burke, Eileen Burke-Sullivan, Phyllis Zagano, editors.
     p.   cm.—(Spirituality in history series)
    Includes bibliographical references.
    ISBN 978-0-8146-1913-1
    1. Ignatius, of Loyola, Saint, 1491–1556. Exercitia spiritualia.   2. Spirituality—Catholic Church.   3. Catholic Church—Doctrines.   4. Spiritual exercises.
I. Burke, Kevin F.   II. Burke-Sullivan, Eileen.   III. Zagano, Phyllis.

BX2179.L8I495   2009
271'.53—dc22

2009021208

In memory of
Fr. James M. Burke, s.j.
(1921–1995)

Contents

Acknowledgments

Excerpts from *A Pilgrim's Journey: The Autobiography of Ignatius of Loyola*. Translated by Joseph N. Tylenda. Wilmington, DE: Michael Glazier, 1985. Copyright Ignatius Press, San Francisco, CA. Reprinted with permission.

Excerpts from *The Spiritual Exercises of Saint Ignatius: A Translation and Commentary*. Translated by George E. Ganss. St. Louis, MO: The Institute of Jesuit Sources, 1992. Used with permission: © The Institute of Jesuit Sources, St. Louis, MO. All rights reserved.

Excerpts from *The Constitutions of the Society of Jesus*. Translated by George E. Ganss. St. Louis, MO: The Institute of Jesuit Sources, 1970. Used with permission: © The Institute of Jesuit Sources, St. Louis, MO. All rights reserved.

Excerpts from *Till God Will: Mary Ward Through Her Writings*. Edited by M. Emmanuel Orchard. London: Darton, Longman and Todd, 1985. Reprinted with permission.

Excerpt from *Instructions on Prayer*. Unpublished manuscript from MHSI. Translated by Martin O'Keefe. Vol. 4. St. Louis, MO: The Institute of Jesuit Sources. Used with permission: © The Institute of Jesuit Sources, St. Louis, MO. All rights reserved.

Excerpt from Joseph Conwell, *Walking in the Spirit*. St. Louis, MO: The Institute of Jesuit Sources, 2003. Used with permission: © The Institute of Jesuit Sources, St. Louis, MO. All rights reserved.

Excerpt from Thomas Clancy, *The Conversational Word of God*. St. Louis, MO: The Institute of Jesuit Sources, 1978. Used with permission: © The Institute of Jesuit Sources, St. Louis, MO. All rights reserved.

Excerpts from Joseph DeGuibert, *The Jesuits: Their Spiritual Doctrine and Practice*. Edited by George Ganss. Translated by William Young. St. Louis, MO: The

1988 by Harper & Row Publishers, Inc. Reprinted by permission of HarperCollins Publishers.

Excerpts from *The Phenomenon of Man* by Pierre Teilhard de Chardin. Translated by Bernard Wall. Introduction by Julian Huxley. Copyright 1955 by Editions de Seuil. Translation and Introduction copyright 1959 by William Collins Sons & Co. Ltd. and Harper & Brothers; copyright renewed 1987 by Harper & Row Publishers, Inc. Reprinted by permission of HarperCollins Publishers.

Excerpt from Pierre Teilhard de Chardin, *Toward the Future*. Translated by René Hague. New York: Harcourt Brace Jovanovich, 1975. Reprinted with permission.

Excerpt from Pierre Teilhard de Chardin, *Hymn of the Universe*. New York: Harper & Row Publishers Inc., 1965. Reprinted with permission of Georges Borchardt, Inc.

Excerpt from *The Making of a Mind: Letters from a Soldier-Priest, 1914–1919* by Pierre Teilhard de Chardin. Copyright ©1961 by Editions Bernard Grasset. English translation Copyright © 1965 by William Collins Sons & Co., Ltd., London, and Harper & Row, Inc., New York, p. 57. Reprinted with permission of Georges Borchardt, Inc., for Editions Bernard Grasset.

Excerpts from *Insight: A Study of Human Understanding* by Bernard Lonergan. Fifth Edition. Toronto, CN: University of Toronto Press, 1993. Reprinted with permission.

Excerpts from *A Second Collection* by Bernard Lonergan. Edited by William F. J. Ryan and Bernard J. Tyrrell. Philadelphia: Westminster Press, 1974 (reprinted with permission for USA); Toronto, CN: University of Toronto Press, 1993 (reprinted with permission for Canada).

Excerpt from "Ignatius of Loyola Speaks to a Jesuit Today," by Karl Rahner. Unpublished translation by J. Matthew Ashley. The German is found in *Schriften zur Theologie XV, Wissenschaft und christlicher Glaube*. Zürich: Benziger, 1984. Reprinted with permission.

Photo reproductions of the Daniel Seghers, s.j., painting *Madonna and Child with Garlands* (seventeenth century; oil on canvas) used with permission: © The Jesuit School of Theology at Berkeley, Berkeley, CA. All rights reserved.

Excerpt from *Images of Faith: An Exploration of the Ironic Imagination* by William F. Lynch. Notre Dame, IN: University of Notre Dame Press, 1973. Reprinted with permission.

Excerpts from *Images of Hope: Imagination as Healer of the Hopeless* by William F. Lynch. Baltimore, MD: Helicon Press, Inc., 1965. © New York Province of the Society of Jesus. Reprinted with permission.

will publish the official version of the proceedings of General Congregation 35 in a subsequent volume. www.jesuitsources.com. Reprinted with permission.

Excerpt from Adolfo Nicholás, "Homily of the New Father General at the Mass of Thanksgiving" (January 21, 2008). Creighton University Online Ministries, http://www.creighton.edu/CollaborativeMinistry/GC35/CG35_2008-01-20%20 Homily_eng.pdf. Copyright Jesuit Conference of the United States, 2008. Reprinted with permission.

Preface

The worldwide explosion of interest in "spirituality" has sent inquirers in several directions. One of the more fruitful is toward the traditional spiritualities that have enriched and nurtured the church for many hundreds of years. Among the oldest Christian spiritualities are those connected to particular foundations, charisms, or individuals. This series of spiritualities in history focuses on five distinct traditions within the history of the church, those now known as Benedictine, Carmelite, Dominican, Franciscan, and Ignatian.

Each volume in the series seeks to present the given spiritual tradition through an anthology of writings by or about persons who have lived it, along with brief biographical introductions of those persons. Each volume is edited by an expert or experts in the tradition at hand.

The present volume of Ignatian spirituality has been coedited by Kevin F. Burke, s.j., and Eileen Burke-Sullivan, both experts in Ignatian spirituality. Father Burke is associate professor of systematic theology and dean of the Jesuit School of Theology at Berkeley, California. He is author of several other works, including *The Ground Beneath the Cross: The Theology of Ignacio Ellacuría* (Georgetown University Press, 2000), *Love that Produces Hope: The Thought of Ignacio Ellacuría*, with Robert Lassalle-Klein (Liturgical Press, 2006), and *Pedro Arrupe: Essential Writings* (Orbis Books, 2004). Doctor Burke-Sullivan is assistant professor of pastoral and systematic theology and director of the master of arts in ministry program at Creighton University, Omaha, Nebraska.

Their compact presentation of the essentials of the Ignatian tradition traces the bright spark of Ignatius' genius chronologically and thematically through the four and a half centuries since he codified the methodology of *The Spiritual Exercises* that now serves as a touchstone for the thousands of his followers who have found and continue to find God in all things.

The lives and writings of the men and women in this volume—most but not all members of the Society of Jesus—show how remarkable and dedicated Christians lived St. Ignatius' vision of contemplatives in action. Each entry adds another bold color to the picture of Ignatian spirituality, writ large in the continual unfolding of history of the church and of the world.

My own work on this book and for this series has continued with the able assistance of librarians, particularly the reference and interlibrary loan staff of Hofstra University, Hempstead, New York, who have tirelessly met so many of my research needs. I am grateful as well for the congenial staff of Liturgical Press, and especially for the professional support and encouragement of Hans Christoffersen, editorial director, and Peter Dwyer, director of Liturgical Press.

Phyllis Zagano
December 31, 2008
Feast of St. John Francis Regis, s.j.

Introduction

Early in the twenty-first century, in the largely secularized culture of the United States and throughout the English-speaking world, the term "spirituality" is used astonishingly often and with a breadth of definition so inclusive as to be elusive, so capable of meaning anything as to become almost meaningless. Thus the phrase "the Ignatian tradition," while virtually synonymous with "Ignatian spirituality," serves the useful purpose of linking the discussion of particular spiritual practices to the concrete history that produced them. One speaks of tradition, after all, in terms of attitudes and behaviors that are recognizable within a series of historical eras—attitudes and behaviors of different people not always identical in specifics, but always identifiable as a pattern.

The Ignatian tradition came into being through the Christian life of grace granted to Ignatius of Loyola, a sixteenth-century Basque nobleman who abandoned his life of a wealthy courtier to become a means of grace for men and women of many cultures, languages, and vocations. It is as vital now, half a millennium later, as it ever has been. Pope Benedict XVI highlighted the distinctive gifts of the Ignatian tradition to the church, above all, the gift of the Spiritual Exercises of St. Ignatius, in his trenchant remarks to General Congregation 35 of the Society of Jesus in February 2008:

> The Spiritual Exercises are the fountain of your spirituality and the matrix of your Constitutions, but they are also a gift that the Spirit of the Lord has made to the entire Church: it is for you to continue to make it a precious and efficacious instrument for the spiritual growth of souls, for their initiation to prayer, to meditation, in this secularised world in which God seems to be absent.[1]

The Ignatian tradition flows through the life of the Society of Jesus, through at least thirty-four international religious communities of women shaped by this charism,[2] and through the lives of countless laypeople who find their spiritual companionship in Christian Life Community and other Jesuit/lay partner ministries, communities, and organizations throughout the world. It is alive too in communities of other Christian denominations, and even is beginning to shape the lives of men and women in the other great world religions.

As with the other major spiritual traditions in Christian history, the Ignatian tradition will be initially understood by reviewing the life and writings of the practical romantic who gave his name to the pattern. But to grasp this spiritual way as a tradition we must examine the lives and thoughts of others who through the centuries shaped their Christian lives after his. To that end the pages of this book combine a collection of brief biographies with a sampling of evocative writings by men and women who represent professionals at the Ignatian way of life. Each of the voices presented here has formally professed in a public way that this pattern of spirituality shapes his or her journey through human life into death. Most of the voices in this collection are Jesuits; two are women, a vowed religious and a laywoman.

The voices span five centuries of history, beginning with Ignatius and three of his early companions, Pierre Favre, Francis Xavier, and Jerome Nadal. Also included are a brief biography and writings of an Englishwoman, Mary Ward, who attempted against all odds to establish a women's community similar to the Jesuits, inspired by Jesuit guidance, but independent of the Society of Jesus. The lives and writings of Xavier, Roberto de Nobili, and Antonio Ruiz de Montoya dramatically illustrate the missionary character of Ignatian spirituality, and the stunning degree of freedom and adaptability that the Ignatian tradition gives its practitioners in the face of new worlds and new cultures that awaited the Good News of God's saving mercy. The literary, artistic, philosophical, theological, mathematical, and scientific contributions of Gerard Manley Hopkins, Daniel Seghers, Pierre Teilhard de Chardin, William Lynch, Bernard Lonergan, Karl Rahner, and Ignacio Ellacuría exemplify the pursuit of the *magis* in a wide variety of scholarly and artistic enterprises in the modern period. Ellacuría, Edmund Campion, and Alfred Delp lived, worked, wrote, and violently died while witnessing to the magnanimity of the cross in the midst of the madness of violently corrupted political systems. In response to the Second Vatican Council, Pedro Arrupe, the twenty-eighth superior general of the Society of Jesus, Josée Gsell, the laywoman who helped reorganize the Christian Life Communities, and George Ganss, a scholar of the history and spiritual roots of the Ignatian tradition, join the collective voices of recent Jesuit general congregations to give a sense of the direction that Ignatian spirituality is tending in both understanding and practice today. The afterword features the voices of the newest Jesuit general and the most recent general congregation.

Undoubtedly there will be readers who wonder why certain voices are included in such a small collection and, perhaps more insistently, why certain voices are omitted. Many famous Jesuits are not represented here, including most of the Jesuit saints. There are artists, missionaries, musicians, architects, scientists, writers, and a host of Ignatian but non-Jesuit religious and laypeople whose important voices are not presented here. It was never the plan of this book to attempt to say everything about the Ignatian tradition—if that were even possible. Nor is it the purpose of this short text to say that these are the best examples of Ignatian spirituality. Rather, our aim is to present representative figures, men and women living across a wide range of historical contexts and engaging in a variety of works and endeavors. One notices that all of these figures shared these traits in common: they read the signs of their times with an Ignatian perspective and responded with the freedom of the third degree[3] of humility and the generosity of the *magis*.

Throughout this book we aim to present these representatives of the Ignatian tradition in a way that makes them as accessible as possible. For this reason, we occasionally modernize usages that would otherwise be misleading, and, in accordance with current practice, we have used gender-inclusive language wherever possible. We use citations and endnotes sparingly to clarify changes we have made, to explain unusual problems with translations or editions we are citing, and to identify those who assisted us with particular chapters.

In telling the stories of these Ignatian witnesses and gathering this collection of their writings we have been blessed to have had suggestions and support from many Jesuit and lay friends and colleagues. We are indebted to all of them and grateful for their interest and ideas. While we could not name every one of these advisors, we do want to particularly thank Fr. John Padberg, s.j., of the Institute of Jesuit Sources in St. Louis, for sharing his expansive wisdom of the Ignatian tradition when we sought his advice. We are also deeply grateful to Dr. Mary Kuhlman of Creighton University and Ms. Jessica Mueller of the Jesuit School of Theology at Berkeley for their help in reading and correcting drafts, assisting with the numerous finishing details of the book, and serving as helpful eyes, ears, and hands. We thank Phyllis Zagano, our series editor, for the invitation to work with her and for her patience, guidance, and editorial expertise. Likewise, we are indebted to the thoughtful and talented editorial staff at Liturgical Press.

Kevin expresses special thanks to his Jesuit and lay colleagues at the Jesuit School of Theology in Berkeley and his companions in the Missouri Province of the Society of Jesus. Eileen offers her deep gratitude to Michael Sullivan, husband and closest friend. Finally, as brother and sister, we dedicate this book to our uncle, Fr. James Burke, s.j. Father Jim was not only the first Jesuit we ever met; he was a gifted director of the spiritual exercises through whom we first came to know and love Ignatius as our own "friend in the Lord."

The Ignatian Tradition

1 555. The governing house of a new religious order in Rome. Two men sit in the sun on a balcony outside the room of the older man, the superior of the new order. Growing ever more crippled with the passing of the years, he limps back and forth still full of fire, laughing occasionally as he tells his tales. He stops pacing, eyes focusing far away. His voice softens, slows, fills with awe as he tells the story of "the pilgrim"—his own story—and the kindness with which God treated him.

The younger man, a Portuguese priest recently arrived in Rome, listens attentively. His eyes are poor so he squints at his elder pacing back and forth. He has a memory for every detail of cadence and content. Indeed, it was for this reason he was chosen as the older man's recorder. After a time he rises and leaves the old man to his work. He hastens to his own room to write down what he has heard. His personal additions and comments are few, clarifications consigned to the margins. It is the old man's story he tells, for the sake of those who follow him with love.

Such might have been the scene during the month of March as spring cloaked the hills of Rome in a green verdure visible from the balcony, or again, in the fall of that year when the story was resumed after the older priest recovered from a summer-long illness.[1]

In his last years, Ignatius of Loyola, founder and first superior general of the new Society of Jesus had been coaxed and pressured into disclosing the details of his personal transformation from a worldly caballero in the court of Charles V into a companion of the risen Christ eager to bring about the reign of God in his world and time. So loathe was Ignatius to talk about himself, that even after he agreed to give an account of his life for the sake of his companions he refused to write it himself, but agreed to tell it to a companion in the third person voice, identifying himself only as "the pilgrim."

Luis Gonçalves da Câmara, a young Jesuit who was nearly blind but possessed of phenomenal memory, helped Ignatius to compose his *Autobiography*. Begun during the late summer of 1553, the work was interrupted by travels assigned to Gonçalves during most of 1554. In the spring of 1555 they picked up the narrative, but were interrupted by Ignatius' ill heath that summer. They resumed their work with renewed urgency in September and October. Gonçalves returned to Portugal in late October as Ignatius' emissary on an urgent mission and the beloved general died the following July, shortly before Gonçalves returned to Rome. Most of the text of the *Autobiography* was read over by Ignatius before his death, and he seemed content with the younger man's precise memory of the spoken account, so the Jesuit order has long credited the text as authoritative in describing the events narrated as Ignatius remembered them. Gonçalves later wrote his own *Memoriale*, a spiritual journal, which contains additional information about both the process and the men.

From the *Autobiography* we glean many important insights into Ignatius' personal spiritual formation. We can practically hear Ignatius' voice narrate the important steps in his spiritual development such as his brief description of his vigil at the altar of the Madonna at Montserrat:

> On the eve of the feast of Our Lady in March, at night in the year 1522, he went as secretly as he could to a beggar and, stripping off all his garments, he gave them to the beggar. He dressed himself in his chosen attire and went to kneel before the altar of our Lady. At times in this way and at other times standing, with his pilgrim's staff in his hand, he spent the whole night. [2]

From his remembrances we can appreciate the journey by which he grew into a contemplative in action. Likewise, we see how he handed on the experience of his journey through the formal process of the Spiritual Exercises. Through the Exercises, Ignatius attracted and formed the men who became his first companions in the Society of Jesus. His own human story thus contains the primary elements of the tradition that bears his name.

The Biographical Roots of the Ignatian Tradition

Ad majorem Dei gloriam, a favorite phrase of Ignatius, emerged from the heart of medieval ideals of honor and glory that had shaped his early ambition, but had then been purified in the fires of mystical love. Literally translated "to the greater glory of God," the phrase provides a summary statement that, like hypertext in the world of computers, springs open when pressed, to reveal a dense description of attitudes and behaviors. This manner of living the Christ life provides one of the great historical spiritualities found within the Christian tradition. In relationship to the major historical spiritualities of the monastic and the conventual traditions, the Ignatian pattern is the youngest. As such it draws on these earlier methods for living the Christian life but remains distinct from all of them because of its various emphases.

Ignatius Loyola was a man of his own time, but, like Martin Luther with whom he shares the sixteenth-century religious stage, seems to stand above that era. Born in the Basque country of northern Spain in 1491, within months of the completion of the *Reconquista* by Isabella and Ferdinand, and the discovery of the Americas, Ignatius entered history at a moment of extraordinary change in European culture. It was the dawn of Spain's golden age of wealth and power. Initiated by Isabella's material and social support of Christopher Columbus' exploration voyage, this period of extraordinary wealth and power was fueled by the discovery of gold, silver, lands, crops, and slave labor of the peoples of the Americas.

From the larger world of European culture, the Renaissance inaugurated dramatic intellectual growth, as well as strong biblical and spiritual reform in the Spanish Catholic Church. Renaissance thinking set the stage for the Protestant Reformation, which in turn led to the end of Christendom as a united political reality. The printing press, invented only forty years before Ignatius' birth, had already contributed to a revolution of language, literacy, and learning throughout Europe, even while he was a child. In this period of epochal change in Western culture the fundamental theistic worldview of the medieval period gave way to the dawn of an anthropocentric premodernity. Newly formed nations sent ambitious younger sons to unmapped continents where they claimed land and resources in the name of their monarchs, achieving both wealth and power.

In the midst of these momentous cultural quakes, Ignatius discovered a similar tectonic movement within his own heart and mind. He was drawn by circumstance and grace from a life of self glorification to a clear-eyed realism oriented to God's glory. His experience of God's gracious intervention in his personal human struggles, which he learned to carefully observe and methodize, provided the matrix of insights and practices that defined his own spiritual journey and became the foundation for the way of Christian life that is named for him.

Ignatius' Early Life

Ignatius of Loyola was born into a Basque family of clan chiefs and baptized Íñigo, a common name in the Basque language of Euskadi. One of the youngest children in a family of eight boys and three girls, he lost his mother as a small child and his father when he was fifteen. The wife of an older brother cared for him after his mother's death; that same brother inherited the estate and title of Loyola when their father died.

Because of the medieval law of primogeniture and as a younger son in a large noble family, Íñigo had few choices about the direction of his life. He could enlist in the king's army, join in the exploration and conquest in the Americas, enter the service of the church as clergy, or serve one of the lords of the Spanish or imperial court. He had only a minimal education but he learned to read and write in Spanish. Apparently he also received tonsure—the first step toward the clerical state—at the age of thirteen. But after he turned fifteen an undisclosed reversal of fortune sent him to the court of his mother's cousin, Juan Velazquez de Cuellar, the royal treasurer of King Ferdinand and Queen Isabella.

While at court, Íñigo, acquired the style and flourish of a young courtier and began signing his name according to the Latin, Ignatius.[3] He also became enamored of the popular romantic literature of the day: stories of heroic battles, glorious knightly competitions, and the conquest of the hearts of wealthy and beautiful women. He described this period of his life in a single sentence: "Up to the age of twenty-six he was a man given to the vanities of the world; and what he enjoyed most was warlike sport, with a great and foolish desire to win fame."[4]

A French cannonball fired at the small fortified city of Pamplona where he served among the defenders suddenly turned Ignatius' life upside down. From all historical evidence Ignatius had committed himself to a hopeless cause, for the French completely outnumbered the Spanish. His sense of chivalrous honor, however, required him to serve king and country to the end. The cannonball seriously damaged his knee, but the French treated him compassionately. They moved him back to Loyola Castle where family physicians using the primitive surgery of the day did what they could for him. He nearly died after septicemia set in.

As he began to recover Ignatius realized the extent of his injury: a bone protruded near his knee leaving one leg significantly shorter than the other. Unwilling to have either his looks marred or his mobility impaired, Ignatius required the local doctors to saw off the segment that jutted from his knee and reset the bones. Again he endured serious infection and again he barely survived. Aided by tortuous physical therapies that straightened and lengthened the leg, however, he did recover.

During this period of enforced immobility, Ignatius requested books to while away the time and take his mind off the pain. His pious sister-in-law had only two: a popular *Life of Christ* by Ludolph of Saxony (which included significant portions of both the Old and New Testaments) and *Golden Legends,* a collection of saints' lives told in a chivalrous style that captured his imagination and enthusiasm. For over six months Ignatius read, reread, considered, and fantasized about these books. He even copied large segments of both into personal notebooks.

Conversion and the First Steps in Discernment

The Lutheran Reformation caused Catholic authorities in Spain to frown upon vernacular translations of the Bible. Because of this and because he knew no Latin, Ignatius had never read or studied Scripture. Ludolph's *Life of Christ,* however, represented a theological and popular exposition of the doctrines of creation, incarnation, and paschal mystery. It also contained a conflation of the gospel narratives surrounding Jesus' birth, public ministry, and death. Since Ignatius was born and raised in a Catholic family in that most Catholic of countries, the biblical stories provided him with no new data. But having time to read and consider their implications enabled him to experience the truth of the Christian message in an entirely new way. During these months, he ceased to be merely culturally religious and became profoundly faithful.

The *Autobiography* witnesses that from the days of his long physical recovery at Loyola Castle, Ignatius learned to pay careful attention to his affective response to the reading and the fantasies that he wove under the influence of both books. In his imaginary life he entertained himself by daydreams that at one time featured him pursuing and winning a very attractive woman's favor through chivalrous deeds, and at other times described him as a poor and humble servant winning souls for God in the manner of St. Francis or St. Dominic. Both kinds of dreams gave him pleasure in the imagining, but the different states of mind and heart that resulted after spending hours weaving the various fantasies astonished him. When he dreamed of winning human praise and adulation he later felt bored and tired, but when he imagined that he accomplished deeds for God he later felt energized and alive. He told Gonçalves da Câmara that initially he didn't take much note of this, but then a time came when "his eyes were opened a little and he began to marvel at the difference and to reflect upon it."[5]

This first stage of discernment—observing his own thoughts and feelings—led him to begin to address God less through structured formula and instead to practice what he later named a "colloquy." This prayer is an intimate conversation, face-to-face, "in the way one friend speaks to another, or a servant to one in authority—now begging a favor, now accusing oneself of some misdeed, now telling one's concerns and asking counsel about them" (SpEx 54).[6] This very intimate conversational prayer opened his mind and heart to discover the great love that God had for him and the personal interest God took in his choices and in his way of life. This experience of being radically loved and carefully guided compelled Ignatius to leave the comfortable and politically powerful life of a courtier and to seek God's desire for his future. He began a relationship with God that, in these beginning stages, he likened to study with a good teacher who carefully guides his student.

Generally recovered in health, though permanently crippled, Ignatius set out walking on a new path—a path toward living in a way more fully responsive to God's desires for him. Years later Ignatius would call himself the pilgrim—the one on the journey toward God—on the *way* of companioning Jesus. He determined to visit Jerusalem, but he stopped on the way and dwelt for almost a year in a cave near the town of Manresa, Spain, down a steep hill from the Benedictine monastery of Montserrat.

The Months at Manresa

In this setting Ignatius spent hours in prayer accompanied by rigorous physical penances that occasionally left him near death from the extreme privation of food, sleep, and shelter. His impulse was at least in response to the medieval influence, undertaking an overwhelming challenge to prove his worth and his devotion. Later he judged that such efforts may not necessarily have been guided by God, but could well have been responses to a more arrogant spirit of pride where he wanted to "outdo" the giants of medieval spirituality, Francis and Dominic. During these periods of severe self-deprivation he often suffered intense bouts of scrupulosity and an obsessive guilt about his past that seemed to reject the power of God's mercy to forgive him. He even spiraled toward suicide at least once during this period. He later actively discouraged his followers from imitating this extreme penitential behavior, and suggested that they carefully discern the reasons for wanting to. It became clear to him that the matter of doing penance had to be an individual response of love, not an effort to achieve God's love or attention. There should be no uniform expectation of certain ascetical acts required of all because each person is called to demonstrate love uniquely.

Once he discovered that his impulse toward severe penances and the scrupulosity that afflicted him were not from God, he set the penitential behavior aside, the scruples subsided, and he began to live a somewhat more ordered life. At this point he was granted a series of mystical graces, which he later described in his autobiographical account. These graces altered his understanding of his human nature, of God, and of God's desire for his responsive love and service. He understood better his own dissolute history, and received God's absolving mercy. He experienced himself as freed, by God's grace, to seek and discover that which is truly of God. Conversely, he understood in a new way how self-destructive was his former attraction to sin.

Ignatius uses the classical phrase "the discernment of spirits" to name the process of distinguishing between "movements" toward God's desires and "movements" toward his own sinful self-will. While the phrase was not new (numerous discussions about the necessity and practice of discernment appear in the New Testament and throughout the tradition), Ignatius made a striking contribution to this tradition: a psychologically sound and spiritually astute methodology for individual discernment of spirits and discernment of God's will.

The ability to sort among the various attractions in one's life and to discover a concrete expression of God's desires within one's talents and history is based on a graced freedom from compulsions, addictions, or inordinate attachments of all kinds. Ignatius' mystical experience taught him that such freedom is ultimately based on an interior knowledge that God is both the source of all creation and the summit of all our genuine desires. He was convinced that each human person is created for a relationship with God and that all things and relationships given to each person are given to assist in the journey back toward God. Indeed, the purpose of human existence is to respond in freedom to the God of love. This knowledge serves as the foundation of a Christian spiritual life. Without a firm grounding in this first "principle and foundation" (SpEx 23) one cannot fruitfully pursue the spiritual journey.

Rooted in Ignatius' experiences in Manresa, the *Spiritual Exercises* move from this foundation to a series of meditations on the nature of sin and God's redeeming grace. Beginning with sin itself in macrocosmic terms, Ignatius narrowed the focus to meditations on the patterns of sin and weakness in each human life. He recognized that unless one experiences repentance, sin ultimately leads to eternal alienation from God and God's goodness. Therefore, the recognition that one has participated in disrupting God's ordered plan of love along with feelings of sorrow for collaborating in such destruction is sheer grace. Seemingly, for many Christians, that recognition alone enables them to live reasonable Christian lives thereafter. But some, including Ignatius himself, experience the call to do greater things in the service of Christ and the reign of God.

He invited such persons to move, even as he did, into a second phase of spiritual maturity. In this phase he was drawn to contemplate the life events of the mission, sufferings, and death of Jesus, and of the glory of the Lord's resurrection. His prayer involved imagining himself present within the events recounted in the biblical texts he had so carefully copied from Ludolph's *Life of Christ*. His contemplation of the mysteries of Christ formed a doorway through which he entered experientially into the Lord's human life. Given a series of extraordinary graces, or "consolations," he encountered the mystery of Jesus' human and divine reality, the gift of Christ's presence in the Eucharist, and the role of Mary in the church. The climax of Ignatius' experiences at Manresa occurred on the banks of the Cardoner River near the town. He received a graced insight so profound that he understood the created order, the mysteries of faith, and his relationship to God with such clarity that he later said if he added up every grace he ever received from God through his entire life it would not equal the clarity and completeness of those few moments. In the course of these eleven months of purification and enlightenment, his deepest desire shifted. Instead of a life of solitude and penance he now sought a life filled with the apostolic purpose of "helping souls" the way he had been helped.

Years of Study and Ordination

Leaving Manresa with this conviction of call and his desire to respond, Ignatius first fulfilled an earlier commitment to go on pilgrimage to Jerusalem. Once there he was tempted to stay and try to convert Muslims, but the Franciscans in charge sent him back to Europe in order to keep a precarious peace with the Muslim authorities. This pilgrimage was particularly important because it helped Ignatius gain a memory of the physical place of Jesus' life in the world. For the rest of his life he would be able to imagine Jesus on earth more poignantly because he had a capacity to "compose the place" of an encounter in his memory and imagination. The use of these mental faculties was important to Ignatius. They are the personal doorways through which God's Spirit works on the consciousness and affections of the individual disciple.

Returning to Spain he discovered other men and women who were hungry for a deeper spiritual life. He guided them through a series of prayer exercises based on his notes. This ministry brought him face-to-face with the Spanish Inquisition and forced him to experience imprisonment for brief periods as he awaited trials. He was tried and found innocent. Nevertheless, the religious authorities ordered him to limit, and in some cases cease, his work. He soon realized that, given the structures of the medieval Spanish church, he could not fulfill his mission from God unless he became a vowed religious or an ordained priest. Uncertain about finding the right religious community he opted to prepare for the priesthood. In his midthirties he enrolled in Latin, studying with preadolescent boys.

A year later, with the goal of ordination to the priesthood firmly in mind, he studied philosophy and theology at the Spanish universities in Alcalá, Barcelona, and Salamanca. In each of these cities he engaged in spiritual conversations and gave his Spiritual Exercises to men and women, clergy and laity, always inviting others to discover the interior freedom he had come to know. The inquisitors of each city, however, continued to harass him. Finally, he left Spain and matriculated at the University of Paris to complete his religious training.

At every stage of his formation into the priesthood he begged for his daily bread and for enough resources to pursue his studies as well to help others pay their tuition. He gave spiritual counsel and guided various people in the Spiritual Exercises. During the Paris years he took extended trips to Flanders and even to England to beg from wealthy patrons there. Many of those he directed became his greatest benefactors while others introduced him to ecclesial authorities capable of providing protection for his studies and his work.

The Founding of the Society of Jesus

Ignatius studied at the University of Paris for seven years. During that time he met the men who eventually joined him in his way of companioning Christ. Among them he discovered yet another crucial dimension of his "way," the treasure of spiritual companionship with others in Christ. He became a master at the art of spiritual conversation. He liked to say that he attempted always to enter through another's door in order to draw that person out through his door. Thus, Ignatius invited his friends to discover the distinctive way God acted directly on and within their own lives.

When he had nearly finished his studies at Paris, he and six companions professed vows together on the Feast of the Assumption in 1534, both the traditional vows of poverty and chastity and then a third vow to either make their way to Jerusalem on a mission to preach the Gospel among the Muslims—if that would be possible within a year—or to go to Rome and place themselves at the direct service of the pope.

These *compañeros*, a company of friends committed to service of God, did not yet see themselves as a religious community. For this reason, they did not profess a vow of obedience to one of their own companions. But when an unusual combination of war, famine, and terrible weather made their mission to Jerusalem impossible, they journeyed to Rome to fulfill their alternative vow. On the way two further events shaped the final form of this "way of Ignatius." The first was a remarkable vision of God the Father and Jesus carrying his cross that came to Ignatius while he was praying at a wayside shrine at La Storta. In the context of the vision the Father turned to Jesus and asked him to take Ignatius as companion and servant. God then told Ignatius that God would guide and support him and his companions in Rome. Quite reasonably, the companions took this profound experience of their leader as a sign of God's blessing on the group, on their choice of the name Society of Jesus, and on their commitment to apostolic service to the whole church. For Ignatius it was a confirmation of the companionship and their common call to help souls through preaching, spiritual conversation, and giving the Spiritual Exercises.

The second singular occurrence was an activity that the companions undertook among themselves in relationship with God and each other. Over the course of the next three months, while engaged apostolically in ministries of teaching, preaching, and consoling the sick, they met together in a process of focused deliberation to discern whether to bind themselves to one another and effectively become a new religious community. They also took up a related but more problematic question as to whether to make a vow of obedience to one of their number. This so-called Deliberation of 1539 became a classic model of corporate decision making. The men committed themselves to hours of prayer, extensive fasting, and other penances. They pondered the situation and needs of the world. They spent long hours sharing with one another their deepest desires, fears, spiritual consolations, and desolations. In the end they determined, with great joy and peace, that God was calling them to form a religious community. Likewise, in addition to their previous vows of poverty, chastity, and service to the Holy Father, they agreed to take a vow of obedience to one of their companions. This deliberation gave birth to the Society of Jesus.

Almost immediately after this decision some members of the group took up residence in Rome while others assumed missions to other parts of Europe. New opportunities to proclaim the Gospel soon followed in the recently discovered worlds of the Americas and Asia. Pope Paul III formally approved their petition to found a new order in 1540. Ignatius, but for his own vote, was elected the first general. He remained in Rome for the last sixteen years of his life, overseeing the initial growth of the new order, composing the *Formula of the Institute* and, with the help of his secretary, Juan de Pulanco, eventually writing the *Constitutions* of the Society of Jesus.

Principles of Ignatian Spirituality

We have rehearsed the story of Ignatius' life as the immediate source of the Ignatian tradition. But his story by itself does not comprise the complete matrix from which this "way" of living the Christian Gospel emerges. The path of only one person, however laudable, remains simply that if others cannot understand the path and imitate it. As his life story illuminates, almost immediately after his conversion experience Ignatius realized that the graces he received, as well as his struggles to respond to them, were similar to those of others who engaged similar forms of prayer and ascetic practices with generosity and attention.

Ignatius not only guided his companions in his *Spiritual Exercises*, he expected his companions to share, from their own experience, this gift with others. In some cases his companions seemed to understand the dynamic and the "theory" of the process better than Ignatius did. Gradually the guiding book was edited and redacted to include the wisdom and experiences of those other first companions. While there are certain fundamental insights that are drawn from Ignatius himself, the spirituality that emerges from his way is enriched, more deeply understood, and handed on through the lived experience of many others in various languages and cultures, in places as far-flung as Portugal, India, Russia, South Africa, the missions of South America, and the city of Rome. The movement grew through the ensuing five centuries of men and women, religious, clergy, and laity living this tradition. It continues to develop today.

Ignatian spirituality can be understood as a matrix of core principles. These principles manifest in specific behaviors and form a graced dynamic of synergistically interactive coordinates that shape both persons and communities of persons into apostolic witnesses of God's trinitarian presence in history. We identify and briefly describe eight such core principles.

God's a priori Love

The foundation of all Ignatian spirituality is the felt knowledge (described by the Spanish verb *sentir*) of God's a priori love. This is not simply an ideological assent to an assertion that God loves, but is a deeply received psychological knowing, grounded in a graced (i.e., given) experience. A human person cannot confect or pretend the experience that is fundamentally transformative. All Christian spirituality presumes this love, but for Ignatius it became manifest for each person in a recognizable sensibility within each one who receives it and responds to it. For Ignatius this experiential knowing, both intellectual and affective, touches the core of human desire and provides the necessary energy for generous response. This experience of the a priori love of God forms the grace of the "principle and foundation" of the Exercises and of the whole spiritual life for two reasons. First, in its most explicit sense, all Christian spirituality flows from God's first act of creating and redeeming each person. Second, a person's experience of that love undercuts the power of self-loathing, the negative effects of human rejection, and the human tendency to fear death and a myriad of other perceived threats. This experience of a priori love locates a person in right relationship to the sovereignty of God.[7]

This grace provides foundation in a second sense because it establishes an experiential touchstone in the memory of the disciple from which discernment of spirits can proceed. If the retreatant can remember the power of the feeling of God's love for her, that knowledge continues to feed her deepest and truest desires. Further, it clarifies *how* God's grace operates identifiably within this specific human subject. This sensibility to God's presence and love becomes the affective and intellectual foundation for future discernment of spirits.

In most cases the profound experience of being loved by God opens an *exercitant* (one who is in the process of making the Spiritual Exercises or who, by extension, is living out Ignatian spirituality) to receive the graces of the first week: the subject's knowledge of self as both sinner and loved. It is this knowledge of God's love while one is far off and in sin (Eph 2:11-13) that establishes the possibility for a unique call. Finally this grace serves to provide the logical necessity both of responding to such overwhelming love by loving God, and fueling the subject's humble service—about which more is said below.

God's Unique Operation in and with Each Person

The experiential knowing of God's love continues to operate uniquely with each person to lead him to his fullest development as a human person. Ignatius stated that he experienced God working directly in his mind and heart as a schoolmaster leads a student. This direct and immediate activity of God grounds the sensibility of different gifts and vocations that is at the heart of Ignatian spirituality. No "one size fits all." No spiritual or ascetical practice can be prescribed universally. Those guiding the Exercises are instructed in a series of twenty annotations at the very beginning of the book to adapt the process of growth to the specific needs, impedances, and gifts of each person they direct. Throughout the process this personalization continues with various notes, rules, suggestions, and recommendations all directed toward helping the director understand that the person she is guiding is unique before God. Some will move faster than others. Each will desire and request graces unique to her need, mission, and growth. Some will find profit in one meditation or contemplation over another. In every case God's grace is uniquely given but with certain common manifestations of thought and feeling that allow the director to recognize and therefore guide the route of the path being followed by the disciple.

To Be Fully Human Requires Spiritual Freedom

God's Spirit labors within the concreteness of human lives and historical moments to call every person into God's reign of mercy and justice. No one can answer the call to God's reign, however, unless he or she achieves spiritual freedom, that is, the capacity to recognize and accept God's call to fuller humanity. Spiritual freedom always entails interior deliverance and often includes some kind of external liberation. It is characterized by courage in the face of terror, hope in the face of despair, wisdom in the face of ignorance or confusion, and joy in the face of unbearable grief.

Spiritual freedom intellectually recognizes the truth and prompts the will to choose the greater good in various circumstances of life and ministry. Ignatius recognized that spiritual freedom is the characteristic of the human as *imago Dei*, as one made in God's image. It is the freedom to master one's own fears and weaknesses even as Jesus did in the Garden of Gethsemane. Ultimately it is the freedom that springs from being loved and it empowers one to love without compulsion or need. Such freedom is the goal of Ignatius' Spiritual Exercises.

Freedom reaches fruition in each human heart through active cooperation with its impelling movements. Both the Old and New Testaments witness to the liberating will of God and its requirement of a response: the commitment to fight or to labor in the manner of God's compassion and justice. Failure to cooperate with the freedom that God wins for us ensures freedom's loss and augers an even greater enslavement.

Human Life Comes to Fruition through Obedience to God's Will

Because of the great influence of Ludolph's *Life of Christ* during his recovery after Pamplona as well as his subsequent awareness of the conversion of his own will, the dominant Christian virtue for Ignatius was obedience to the will of the Father. Such obedience springs from gratitude. It flowers as the empowerment of spiritual freedom. It spreads out seeking the ultimate good of others. One who genuinely loves cannot will to do the beloved harm. Human logic would point out that with God there can be no mistake about knowing what is the best good for the beloved. So the issue lies in absolutely trusting that there is a God who does know all and loves each of us singularly. This trust is prior to knowing and flourishes even when our human knowledge comes up short. This trust is a grace given to the one who asks with deep desire and a willingness to listen, to obey.

The "Enemy of Human Life" Works to Block Our Freedom, Disrupt Our Obedience, and Undermine Our Humanity

Spiritual freedom, which enables us to be authentically human, is diminished and can even be destroyed by acquiescing to the power of the enemy of human life. For Ignatius, the enemy is any force or power, whether personal or corporate, that works within persons, cultures, or nature to diminish the way of mercy, justice, and compassion.

Human sin gives rise to a history marred by violence, depravity, and weakness. Everyone born into that history faces the threat of becoming enslaved to sin's interior and exterior demands. The book of Genesis provides a biblical reflection on the general experience that we cannot choose what is good for us because we cannot even perceive clearly what is good. Even when we can perceive it, we often lack the will or the courage to do it. And even when we both perceive it and courageously act to accomplish it, we may well act from disordered motivations that undermine the outcome. Our perceptions are dulled, our desires are distorted, and our intentions corrupted. This is our condition without grace.

Despite this dark reality of human brokenness and sin, God's power is always greater than any capacity of the enemy to harm the created order, for our real enemies are not divine powers but creatures who have failed to love God. With the assistance of God's Spirit the enemy is overcome. This is true in the case of external forces enslaving whole populations or interior addictions driving one person to self-destruction. With our cooperation, God's Spirit restores spiritual freedom and often material freedom.

Finding God in All Things

The way of Ignatius is essentially incarnational. Ignatius was clearly a man who read the signs of his times and responded to the world he was born into. He did so with the best tools he could find or forge. Ignatius did not look for God to work magic on the world. He never sought a *deus ex machina*. But he did find the presence of God manifest in every aspect of the created order. Too often in the Catholic experience, spirituality has been thought of as doing something pious, praying a rosary, or going to Mass. Ignatian spirituality does not deny the importance of intentional prayer activities, but it is more essentially about recognizing the presence and the power of God in absolutely everything and in every activity done for love. All the created order is overflowing with the divine existence. So the story is remembered of Ignatius going out each night on a balcony at the Roman College and doffing his hat in reverence to the God who created the stars. He knew that all of creation was holy.

In a particular way, Ignatius wanted those who followed him to understand that God is to be found in places where we are least comfortable looking for him. In his human life, Jesus faced the darkest dimensions of human evil and submitted willingly to its power in order that

God's reign might be unleashed and made manifest in the world. Becoming a true companion of Jesus requires following him even when the way leads to crosses large and small. One might find God's presence in the decision of a superior who does not understand his gifts, talents, or vision; one finds God in suffering and illness as much as in good health; one encounters God in disappointments as much as in success. One finds God even in the failure of God's own project. All that is human, all that springs from the body, mind, and spirit, springs from God and for God.

God is not "more" present in a church than a courtroom, a monastery than an operating room, but God is found differently in each human context. God is present in and to every aspect of our human living and loving. In this spiritual tradition one can discover God's presence in the groans of a dying old man as in the whispered prayers of the young novice. There is nothing inherently holier in spending time in the presence of the Blessed Sacrament than there is in spending time teaching algebra to high school sophomores. There is nothing inherently more graced about saying the rosary than there is about fixing supper for one's husband and children. Studying theology is not necessarily holier than working as a laborer, clerk, or executive. God is fully present in every molecule of the universe. The challenge is to find God where God is and not where we think God ought to be. Ignatian spirituality teaches that the essence of the spiritual life entails the moment-by-moment search for God's desires throughout the course of one's life.

An Apostolic Focus

Generally for those called by God to Ignatian spirituality, action in the world on behalf of God's reign, according to one's vocation and one's talents, is imperative. What Ignatius called the desire to "help souls" was the ground for an apostolic approach to the world beyond any cloister or church building. In European religious practice of the sixteenth century this was unusual for vowed religious communities. Even lay organizations were often pious prayer societies. Today such apostolic focus represents a major theme for religious life due, in large part, to the pioneering work of Ignatius and his companions. As early as the twelfth century, Francis of Assisi and Dominic Guzman had seen the necessity for a ministry of preaching, hearing confessions, and responding to human needs in the highways and byways of medieval Europe beyond the convent and cloister. Even so, their rules called for extended and established times for prayer, often sung in choir as generations of monks had done before them.

Ignatius did not replicate monastic practice when he and his companions determined to form a religious community. They saw themselves called above all to direct service of the Gospel in the streets of cities where humanity dwells in poverty, ignorance, and often violence. If one is faithful, attentive, and generous in redressing the greatest or most demanding needs to which he is sent, the labor itself, whether spiritual, material, intellectual, or social, and the relationships that arise from such service, provide both an encounter with the risen Lord and any necessary penance and self-abnegation. Formal prayer is limited to short periods of meditation each day, regular participation in Eucharist and reconciliation, and daily times of self-examination to discern whether one is following the light of consolation from God or desolation from darker impulses. This discerning examination focuses not only on interior movements of formal prayer but especially on the movements and impulses that occur during and within the daily activities of apostolic life and all human interactions. Holiness comes from an intimacy with God through partnership with Jesus in obediently discerned service of others.

Companionship in and with Christ

Despite some historic accusations that followers of Ignatius are "lone rangers," in the work of spreading the Gospel an important sensibility of Ignatian spirituality is the necessity for companionship in prayer, in service, in the struggle for justice, in the works of mercy, indeed in all aspects of life. The first companion is Jesus Christ, but Jesus' closest companions become guides, friends, and partners in the mission. The Spiritual Exercises are to be undertaken under the guidance of a spiritual companion. In the meditation on the two standards from the second week the retreatant recognizes the deep friendship among the servants of the Lord that characterizes those who rally under the standard of Christ. The word "companion" comes from the Spanish verb "to [have] bread with" and with it we are reminded that much of Jesus' ministry of reconciliation and implementation of the reign of God in the world comes through the mediation of table fellowship. Companions are those who will not only walk the extra mile with you, but labor in the hot sun through the middle of the day and have a cold beer and hear your stories around the fire; or teach all day in the next classroom and then share a hot cup of tea with tales of the (mis)adventures of the mission. Companionship is also an extension of the great love shared with those serving the same Lord in a project far away in another land, culture, and language—the sense that those who follow this pattern of Gospel life are "ours."

Ignatian Practices

In addition to the matrix of core principles that distinguish Ignatian spirituality, Ignatius and his first companions developed a collection of basic practices that help to realize in each person's life the essential principles described above. These practices are not rigid; nor are they absolute for every person who wants to live the Gospel in this way. They are better seen as a set of tools that can be effectively employed to open the heart, mind, and will of the Christian to receive God's direction, and to become interiorly free and willing to be sent to the most effective labor of God's reign. We focus here on five basic practices that give shape to Ignatian spirituality.

Imaginative Prayer

Methods of prayer that progressively lead to the discovery of, and eventual cooperation with, God's actions within each person provide the driving energy of Ignatian spirituality. The forms of prayer Ignatius recommended for those undergoing the Spiritual Exercises are ordinarily incarnational or imagistic. These methods involve the whole range of intellectual capacities: memory, imagination, intuition, ability to reflect, and logical reasoning. They also engage the entire physical capacity to experience reality through the senses and the use of various postures in order to embody praise, sorrow, wonder, or need.

In the specific prayer called the "application of the senses," Ignatius instructs directors of the Exercises to encourage their exercitants to "see with the eyes of the imagination the synagogues, villages, and towns where Christ our Lord preached" (SpEx 91),[8] "to see the different persons, first, those on the face of the earth, in such great diversity in dress and in manner of acting . . . see and consider the Three Divine Persons seated on the royal dais or throne of the Divine Majesty . . . see our Lady and the angel saluting her" (SpEx 106). Likewise, he bids one "to listen to what the persons on the face of the earth say, that is how they speak to one another, swear and blaspheme . . . also hear what the Divine Persons say . . . listen to what the angel and our lady say" (SpEx

107). Most significantly, he urges the retreatant not only to see and hear but to put himself in the story. Thus, in the contemplation on the nativity, after seeing all the persons in the story, the exercitant is encouraged to consider herself "a poor little unworthy slave, and as though present, look upon [the Holy Family], contemplate them, and serve them in their needs with all possible homage and reverence" (SpEx 114). This application of the senses requires the person to bring the affections into focus: the desires, fears, and hopes for the future. Finally, Ignatian prayer calls for the willful responsibility to choose among multiple options that surface.

All of the aspects of the human person are intentionally and deliberately drawn into prayer through the various methods that build upon one another. Through brief but dynamic daily prayer the Ignatian person engages in a generous, lifetime effort to hear and obey God's will, gradually becoming an ever freer and more intimate participant in the Christ life.

Rules for Discernment

Ignatius found, both in his own experience and in the men and women that he guided spiritually, that all were inclined toward or away from God by various exterior coercions and, more forcefully, by inner compulsions, which he described as known or unknown human desires. Beyond basic human needs that allow us to survive, we have an array of wants or desires that are triggered by each person's hope for a better human existence. Questions such as "What do I really want? Who do I want to become? Who do I want to be in relationship with? What do I want to have? How do I want to behave? What is truly meaningful or life-giving for me?" drive human choosing in a way that is not comparable in the rest of the animal kingdom. Responding to these and similar questions establishes a fabric of human existence that is either life-giving or death-dealing for oneself and sometimes for others. Choosing among incompatible desires is often the most difficult human task, but failure to choose can leave a person paralyzed in inaction.

Ignatius called "consolation" those intellectual insights, emotional impulses, invitations, or pulls that led him to love God more deeply and to desire whatever God desires. Conversely, he named "spiritual desolation" the various forms of intellectual darkness that led him to deny the will of God. Possessing wealth, power, security, or any material thing leads a human to being possessed and therefore enslaved to these impulses he defined as desolation. He also recognized ripe occasions for desolation in human fears of death, change, or uncertainty because such fears often paralyze the human spirit.

Based on his own experiences with these and other drives, desires, and impulses Ignatius found he was able to help souls find their true inner freedom by guiding each one to trust God. God works for the radical good of each human life and guides each person within the complex interaction of ideas, emotions, and desires that surface in her life. To this end, Ignatius developed a broad set of very practical rules for determining whether inner movements or impulses come from God (spiritual consolations) or the enemy (spiritual desolation). Cooperating with consolation and working against desolation becomes the task of the spiritual journey into God. Necessarily the rules deal with intellectual processes, emotional experiences, willed decisions, and various actions or behaviors, but at the heart of all discernment is to discover one's deepest and truest desires and the goal(s) they point to. In a reasonably healthy human person such desires are ordered toward one's authentic good—and thus come from and lead toward God.

Generally, Ignatius' rules follow the principle that as one draws closer toward God the enemy works harder to block the graced movement, so the task of discernment becomes more complex. His rules, therefore, are ordered to the stage of the spiritual journey where one actually is located. Furthermore, Ignatius was committed to staying within the ecclesial tradition. He points to the importance of weighing one's personal wisdom against the long practice and insight of the apostolic community of faith even when interpreting that tradition within a new period of human growth. God's Spirit will not act in a manner contrary to the teaching and practice of Jesus as witnessed by the church. He also recognized that choices build one upon another. A Spirit-led choice will not undermine or destroy a previously discerned decision that established a set of committed relationships.

An important experience in Ignatius' life illustrated this insight. After his brushes with the Inquisition in Spain he determined that he needed to be ordained a priest in order to effectively help souls. Further, he had been scandalized often enough by mediocre or poor priests who did great harm to God's people from ignorance of the scriptural, doctrinal, liturgical, and spiritual aspects of the tradition. Ignatius saw that, among other things, effective priests needed to be well educated. For this reason he entered a long process of education from elementary Latin to a master of arts in theology. While he pursued his studies, Ignatius discovered that he had to set aside some of the time given to prayer and even his charitable work to accomplish his goal. He experienced what appeared to be powerful consolations that kept him locked in delightful prayer for hours during the night. Attending to these consolations, however, made it difficult to study or sleep enough to be a competent student. He discerned that the experiences that seemed like consolations from God were in fact leading him away from the apostolic work that God called him to accomplish. This kind of false consolation was not new to him, but it confirmed for him that a seeming good could be the counterfeit of the enemy.

Determining what was graced or disgraced in such times could not be determined solely by the feelings or thoughts that accompanied them, but decisions had to be seen in relationship to the demands of rightly discerned decisions already made. The capacity to discover whether a seeming consolation is in fact that or a movement toward less good or a disguised evil is a gift of God that is urgently necessary for those who have responded to the call of Christ to greater service. Ignatius' more advanced rules indicate that the only way to discover the truth of whether a desire is from God is to prayerfully determine the context of its coming, the goal toward which it seems to lead, and the relationship it has to other decisions. A discerner usually does this best in dialogue with a trained guide who holds no vested interest in the outcome.

Agere Contra (*Practice Working against the Enemy*)

When one following the Ignatian way discovers any manifestation of the enemy blocking her path toward companionship with Jesus, she is instructed to ask for the specific grace needed to counter this power. It may be a grace of patience when the world seems to move too slowly, the grace of courage in the face of fear, or the grace of compassion to deal well with a difficult coworker. One is instructed to name—as a desire to be prayed for—whatever specific grace one needs in a given situation. Furthermore, the person asking for this grace is instructed to act confidently as if the grace is already given. This works against the power of desolation. *Agere contra* in the face of desolation is a generous act of human cooperation that develops strength of will. By practicing it the discerning person works to concretize in his own life the power of God's grace. He develops a kind of spiritual muscle that corresponds to the language of spiritual exercises.

Examen

Accompanying the practice of prayer for a specific desire, Ignatius encouraged one who is seeking to grow in the spiritual life to practice a review of a specified period of time (one's prayer time, or the morning of work, or the whole day) to discover whether the grace desired was granted, whether one practiced *agere contra* successfully, and to ascertain the spirits that moved one to various decisions and actions. This practice of examen becomes established as a habit while a person makes the Exercises. Afterward she will continue the practice each day providing the foundation for ongoing, daily discernment.

After participation in the Eucharist, Ignatius taught that the examen was the most important spiritual practice in the life of a Jesuit. If his mission required him to abandon virtually all other spiritual habits he must not give up the practice of daily examen; those few moments allow him to notice and face the hidden and unbidden impulses that subtly rule human choice if left unexamined. Even a serious disciple of Jesus, if he neglects to examine the movements of interior spirits, often falls prey to the manipulations of the enemy.

Magnanimity: The Magis and Humility

The virtue of generosity is witnessed to the degree that the exercitant remains faithful to prayer, open to the director's guidance, steady in the practice of *agere contra*, generous in forgiving the wrongs of others, and passionate about laboring with Jesus and under his standard. Ignatius insists that one who begins the Exercises must be generous in these ways so that he can receive gifts in greater abundance from God. Beyond generosity, however, is the virtue of magnanimity, or greatness of heart, that causes a person to be the first to volunteer for the hardest job—not because one is masochistic or wants appreciation, but because one loves God and God's work needs doing. In his forgiveness of the prodigal son the father in Jesus' famous parable displays magnanimity. Likewise, the magnanimous include those who attend to the dispossessed at the margins of society and help them find ways to live. A variety of evangelical examples—giving your coat to one who asks for a shirt, walking the extra mile, caring for the injured neighbor on the road, and so on— witness to what Ignatius calls magnanimity.

Such largeness of spirit is rooted in the practice of humility, which is the fruit of gratitude. Like the word "love" in English, humility can have many meanings or shades of meaning. Humility within the Spiritual Exercises describes the grace of living the absolute truth that God is God and that I am not God for myself or anyone else. Further, my whole existence flows from God's generosity, so I owe God everything. I recognize that all I am and all I have is gift of God. Gratitude flows inherently from this experience of God's boundless generosity.

The capstone of the Spiritual Exercises is a contemplation to attain love for God. The meditation is constructed so as to arouse heartfelt gratitude in the exercitant. From gratitude flows humility. From humility flows increased generosity that explodes into magnanimity so profound, that she prays, "Take, Lord, and receive all my liberty; my memory, my understanding, and all my will—all that I have and possess" (SpEx 234).

The exercitant asks that for the rest of his life he will understand that his truest and most glorious existence is to be a loyal servant of God. No rank or wealth or material measure in this life can change these simple facts about human existence. Such graced humility grants the recipient the desire to serve God's reign in the most modest, most dangerous, or most difficult of tasks and at whatever cost might be required. Thus the most humble of all has the greatest and truest heart.

From this spirit of magnanimous love, the follower of the Ignatian tradition will seek to accomplish the most difficult or least sought-after work, that will bring about the greatest good for the greatest number, but in a manner that gives glory to God not self. The term *magis* is applied to this sensibility—to seek the greater glory of God by doing the task no one else wants but that has to be done for the good of many or of all. Finally, a magnanimous person does what he does for love alone without counting the cost or seeking redress for his losses or his suffering.

Summary

In summary, one can approach Ignatian spirituality both by tracing its emergence in the graced experiences of Ignatius of Loyola and by identifying the principles and practices at work when one adopts this way of Christian life. The principles and practices described above are all drawn from the totality of the Christian life, but the interweaving of these coordinates into a specific spiritual DNA causes the one who chooses to be shaped by them (1) to seek the greater glory of God, (2) through companionship with Jesus, and (3) always be guided by the discerned Spirit of God; (4) to seek that greater glory (5) in the reality of this historical moment, (6) in this particular place, (7) within the whole created world. All of this suggests that while the Ignatian tradition attends to the traditional spiritual themes of purgation, illumination, and union, it is best approached as a mysticism of service.

Eileen Burke-Sullivan

PART I
FOUNDATIONS

There can be no doubt that St. Ignatius of Loyola generated the earliest expression of the pattern of insights and practices that bear his name. Likewise, the *Spiritual Exercises* of Ignatius functions as the primary classical text for this spirituality. Ignatius discovered that his experience could be shared with others to evoke their own growth into the life of Christ, and it was his special genius to develop a method or pattern to mediate that sharing.

Another founder within the Ignatian tradition is the lesser-known Englishwoman, Mary Ward. She founded an apostolic religious order for women, modeled on the Society of Jesus, that today has two branches, the Institute of the Blessed Virgin Mary and the Congregation of Jesus. Mary's translation of Ignatius' insights into a pattern of active, communal life for women enabled many to witness to great holiness in the process of serving outside the cloister.

Both Ignatius of Loyola and Mary Ward can be understood to have founded religious institutes, that is, human structures placed at the service of the church and the world. We are here concerned with the foundations of a particular way of living the Gospel of Jesus Christ, a unique Christian tradition of spirituality. Theologically, the true *founder* of the Ignatian spiritual tradition is the Holy Spirit. But God built this tradition on the *foundations*—the life stories, mystical experiences, holy desires, and uncommon talents—of Ignatius and Mary. Thus, their lives and instructions serve as privileged texts for understanding the pattern of grace that God raised up through their cooperation. Likewise, their communities, marked by persecution, suppression, and eventual restoration, nurtured a spiritual tradition that grew and flourished for men and women within and beyond their communities. Our first two chapters focus on these two foundations of the Ignatian tradition.

Eileen Burke-Sullivan

Ignatius of Loyola (1491–1556)

An overview of the life of Ignatius is presented in the essay that introduces this volume, *The Ignatian Tradition*, and need not be sketched here. The selections below taken from *The Autobiography of St. Ignatius* (where Ignatius tells his story in the third person and refers to himself as "the pilgrim") dwell on certain key moments in his life as told in his own words. These include his early experiences with discernment ("Convalescence and Conversion") while he was recovering from a cannonball wound he received while defending the city of Pamplona. They also include Ignatius' description of his two most important mystical experiences, experiences that frame Ignatian spirituality. The first occurred in 1522 near the Cardoner River during his time in Manresa. In the wake of this powerful illumination Ignatius shaped and confirmed all of his foundational spiritual and theological insights. The latter vision occurred in 1537 in the chapel of La Storta on the road outside of Rome where Ignatius and two of his companions were journeying in order to place themselves at the service of the church. This event provided the first companions with a confirmation of their decision to found the Society of Jesus.

Without question the most influential book of Ignatius' is *The Spiritual Exercises*. We include here the first five of twenty important comments that Ignatius offers those who direct and those who make the Exercises ("Introductory Explanations"; SpEx 1–5). This is followed by the brief paragraph known as the "Presupposition" of the Exercises (SpEx 22). It is often overlooked in directing or making the retreat. But one must not overlook it. It instructs the director to recognize that she may be biased in her listening skills—too eager to condemn or correct another's statements. It is as valid and necessary today as the day Ignatius added it to the text. The third selection is the text of a famous meditation that Ignatius calls the "Principle and Foundation" (SpEx 23). Those who direct the Spiritual Exercises today know that this meditation is designed to test whether the person who wishes to make the Exercises has been given the grace to do so by God, the grace of sensing God's foundational a priori love for him or her. One could say that the principle and foundation provides a summary of the graces of the whole retreat—namely, the spiritual freedom that one is seeking in making the Exercises. During preparation days the retreatant is asked to consider what inner spirits this powerful (and very countercultural) assertion arouses in the one wanting to begin the Spiritual Exercises. The final selection from the *Spiritual Exercises* is a portion of the famous "Contemplation to Attain Divine Love" that completes or summarizes the process of the Exercises (SpEx 230–37). This contemplation invites the retreatant to pray deeply for the desire to love God who has so loved him. At the heart of this prayer lies the grace of spiritual freedom that allows him to be utterly indifferent to all but God's identified will in his regard.

During the last years of his life, while administrating the newly established Jesuit order, Ignatius worked with his secretary and friend Juan de Pulanco to develop *The Constitutions for the Society*. The selection included here (from part 9 of *The Constitutions*) concerns the character of the man who is to be elected general of the Society. If anyone is to manifest the character of Ignatian spirituality, it must be the man who leads and guides the fortunes of Ignatius' vowed followers. In this summary of the vision and gifts needed to fulfill the demands of such a critical work Ignatius gives us a glimpse of what his spirituality looks like coming down the street.

Eileen Burke-Sullivan and Kevin F. Burke, s.j.

From *A Pilgrim's Journey: The Autobiography of St. Ignatius*

Convalescence and Conversion (1521–1522)

> By frequent reading of these books he grew somewhat fond of what he found written therein. Setting his reading aside, he sometimes paused to think about the things he had read, and at other times he thought of the worldly things that formerly occupied his mind. Of the many idle things that came to him, one took such a hold on his heart that, without his realizing it, it engrossed him for two or three hours at a time. He dreamed what he would achieve in the service of a certain lady and thought of the means he would take to go to

the land where she lived, the clever sayings and words he would speak to her, and the knightly deeds he would perform for her. He was so enraptured with these thoughts of his that he never considered how impossible it was for him to accomplish them, for the lady was not one of the lesser nobility, neither was she a countess, nor a duchess, but her station was much higher than any of these.

Our Lord, nevertheless, came to his aid, bringing it about that these thoughts were followed by others arising from his reading. While reading the life of our Lord and those of the saints he used to pause and meditate, reasoning with himself: "What if I were to do what Saint Francis did, or to do what Saint Dominic did?" Thus in his thoughts he dwelt on many good deeds, always suggesting to himself great and difficult ones, but as soon as he considered doing them, they all appeared easy of performance. Throughout these thoughts he used to say to himself: "Saint Dominic did this, so I have to do it too. Saint Francis did this, so I have to do it too." These thoughts lasted a long time, but after other thoughts had taken their place, the above-mentioned worldly ones returned to him and he dwelt on them for quite some length. This succession of such diverse thoughts—of worldly exploits that he desired to accomplish, or those of God that came to his imagination—stayed with him for a long time as he turned them over in his mind, and when he grew weary of them he set them aside to think of other matters.

There was this difference, however. When he thought of worldly matters he found much delight, but after growing weary and dismissing them he found that he was dry and unhappy. But when he thought of going barefoot to Jerusalem and of eating nothing but vegetables and of imitating the saints in all the austerities they performed, he not only found consolation in these thoughts but even after they had left him he remained happy and joyful. He did not consider nor did he stop to examine this difference until one day his eyes were partially opened and he began to wonder at this difference and to reflect upon it. From experience he knew that some thoughts left him sad while others made him happy, and little by little he came to perceive the different spirits that were moving him; one coming from the devil, the other coming from God.[1]

Manresa and the Cardoner River (1522–1523)

During this period God was dealing with him in the same way a schoolteacher deals with a child while instructing him. This was because either he was thick and dull of brain, or because of the firm will that God Himself had implanted in him to serve Him—but he clearly recognized and has always recognized that it was in this way that God dealt with him. Furthermore, if he were to doubt this, he would think he was offending the Divine Majesty. One can see how God dealt with him in the following five examples.

First. He was greatly devoted to the Most Holy Trinity, and every day he prayed to each of the three Persons. But while doing the same to the Most Holy Trinity the thought came to him, why four prayers to the Trinity? But this thought caused him little or no trouble since it was of so little importance. One day, as he was saying the Hours of Our Lady on the monastery's steps, his understanding was raised on high, so as to see the Most Holy Trinity under the aspect of three keys on a musical instrument, and as a result he shed many tears and sobbed so strongly that he could not control himself. Joining in a procession that came out of the monastery, that morning he could not hold back his tears until dinnertime, and after he had eaten he could not refrain from talking, with much joy and consolation, about the Most Holy Trinity, making use of different comparisons. This experience remained with him for the rest of his life so that whenever he prayed to the Most Holy Trinity he felt great devotion.

Second. One day it was granted him to understand, with great spiritual joy, the way in which God had created the world. He seemed to see a white object with rays stemming from it, from which God made light. He neither knew how to explain these things nor did he fully remember the spiritual lights that God had then imprinted on his soul.

Third. It was likewise in Manresa—where he stayed for almost a year, and after experiencing divine consolations and seeing the fruit that he was bringing forth in the souls he was helping—that he abandoned those extremes he had previously practiced and began to cut his nails and hair. One day, while in town and attending Mass in the church attached to the above-mentioned monastery, he saw with inward eyes, at the time of the elevation of the body of the Lord, some white rays coming from above. But after so long a time he is now unable to adequately explain this; nevertheless, he clearly saw with his understanding how our Lord Jesus Christ was present in that most holy Sacrament.

Fourth. During prayer he often, and for an extended period of time, saw with inward eyes the humanity of Christ, whose form appeared to him as a white body, neither very large nor very small; nor did he see any differentiation of members. He often saw this in Manresa; and if he were to say twenty times or forty times, he would not presume to say that he was lying. He saw it again when he was in Jerusalem, and once more when he was on his way to Padua. He has also seen our Lady in similar form, without differentiation of members. These things that he saw at that time fortified him and gave such great support to his faith that many times he thought to himself: if there were no Scriptures to teach us these matters of faith, he would still resolve to die for them on the basis of what he had seen.

Fifth. He was once on his way, out of devotion, to a church a little more than a mile from Manresa, which I think was called Saint Paul. The road followed the path of the river and he was taken up with his devotions; he sat down for a while facing the river flowing far below him. As he sat there the eyes of his understanding were opened and though he saw no vision he understood and perceived many things, numerous spiritual things as well as matters touching on faith and learning, and this was with an elucidation so bright that all these things seemed new to him. He cannot expound in detail what he then understood, for they were many things, but he can state that he received such a lucidity in understanding that during the course of his entire life—now having passed his sixty-second year—if he were to gather all the helps he received from God and everything he knew, and add them together, he does not think they would add up to all that he received on that one occasion.[2]

La Storta (1537)

The companions returned to Venice in the same way that they had gone, that is, on foot and begging their way, but they were divided into three groups, in such a way that each group was made up of different nationalities. There in Venice, those who were not ordained were ordained for Mass, and the nuncio, who was then in Venice and who was later known as Cardinal Verallo, granted them faculties. They were ordained under the title of poverty and everyone took vows of poverty and chastity.

Ships were not sailing to the East that year because the Venetians had broken off relations with the Turks. Seeing that the possibility of sailing was becoming more remote, they dispersed throughout the Veneto region to wait out the year as they had agreed, and if there were no sailing after the year had passed, they would go to Rome.

It fell to the pilgrim to go with Faber and Laínez to Vicenza. There they found a certain building outside the city that had neither doors nor windows. They stayed in it and slept on the bit of straw that they had brought. Twice a day two of them went out to seek alms in that locality and they returned with so little that they could hardly sustain themselves. They usually ate some bread—when they had bread— and the one who stayed at home took care of the cooking. In this way they spent forty days attending to nothing but their prayers.

After the forty days had passed, Master Jean Codure arrived and the four of them decided to begin preaching. All four went to different squares in the city, and at the same hour of the same day they began their sermons by shouting loudly to the people waving their birettas to call them together. These sermons caused much talk in the city and many persons were moved with devotion and abundantly supplied them with all that they materially needed.

During the period that he was in Vicenza, he received many spiritual visions and many rather ordinary consolations (it was just the opposite when he was in Paris), but especially when he began to prepare for his ordination in Venice and when he was getting ready to celebrate Mass. Also during his journeys he enjoyed great supernatural visitations of the kind that he used to have when he was in Manresa. While he was in Vicenza he learned that one of the companions, who was in Bassano, was at the point of death. Though he himself was ill with fever at the time, nevertheless, he started on the trip and walked so energetically that Faber, his companion, could not keep up with him. During that trip God gave him the assurance, and this he told to Faber, that the companion would not die from that illness. After he arrived at Bassano, the sick man was greatly consoled and quickly recovered.

Everyone then returned to Vicenza and all ten were there for some time and some went out begging alms in the towns around Vicenza.

They decided that after a year had passed, and if they still found no passage, they would go to Rome, and the pilgrim too, because the last time the companions had gone there the two men, about whom he had his doubts, had shown themselves most benevolent.

They went to Rome in three or four groups; the pilgrim was with Faber and Laínez, and on this journey God often visited him in a special way.

After he had been ordained a priest, he decided to wait another year before celebrating Mass, preparing himself and praying to our Lady to place him with her Son. One day, a few miles before reaching Rome, while praying in a church, he felt a great change in his soul and so clearly did he see God the Father place him with Christ, His Son, that he had no doubts that God the Father did place him with His Son.[3]

From *The Spiritual Exercises of Saint Ignatius*

1. *Introductory Explanations*

To gain some understanding of the Spiritual Exercises which follow, and to aid both the one who gives them and the one who is to receive them.

The First Explanation. By the term Spiritual Exercises we mean every method of examination of conscience, meditation, contemplation, vocal or mental prayer, and other spiritual activities, such as will be mentioned later. For, just as taking a walk, traveling on foot, and running are physical exercises, so is the name of spiritual exercises given to any means of preparing and disposing our soul to rid itself of all its disordered affections and then, after their removal, of seeking and finding God's will in the ordering of our life for the salvation of our soul.

2. *The Second.* The person who gives to another the method and procedure for meditating or contemplating should accurately narrate the history contained in the contemplation or meditation, going over the points with only a brief or summary explanation. For in this way the person who is contemplating, by taking this history as the authentic foundation, and by reflecting on it and reasoning about it for oneself, can thus discover something that will bring better understanding or a more personalized concept of the history—either through one's own reasoning or insofar as the understanding is enlightened by God's grace. This brings more spiritual relish and spiritual fruit than if the one giving the Exercises had lengthily explained and amplified the meaning of the history. For what fills and satisfies the soul consists, not in knowing much, but in our understanding the realities profoundly and in savoring them interiorly.

3. *The Third.* In all the following Spiritual Exercises we use the acts of the intellect in reasoning and of the will in eliciting acts of the affections. In regard to the affective acts which spring from the

will we should note that when we are conversing with God our
Lord or his saints vocally or mentally, greater reverence is demanded
of us than when we are using the intellect to understand.

4. *The Fourth.* Four Weeks are taken for the following Exercises,
corresponding to the four parts into which they are divided. That
is, the First Week is devoted to the consideration and contemplation
of sins; the Second, to the life of Christ our Lord up to and including
Palm Sunday; the Third, to the Passion of Christ our Lord; and the
Fourth, to the Resurrection and Ascension. To this Week are ap-
pended the Three Methods of Praying. However, this does not mean
that each Week must necessarily consist of seven or eight days. For
during the First Week some persons happen to be slower in finding
what they are seeking, that is, contrition, sorrow, and tears for their
sins. Similarly, some persons work more diligently than others, and
are more pushed back and forth and tested by different spirits. In
some cases, therefore, the Week needs to be shortened, and in others
lengthened. This holds as well for all the following Weeks, while the
retreatant is seeking what corresponds to their subject matter. But
the Exercises ought to be completed in thirty days, more or less.

5. *The Fifth.* The persons who make the Exercises will benefit
greatly by entering upon them with great spirit and generosity
toward their Creator and Lord, and by offering all their desires and
freedom to him so that His Divine Majesty can make use of their
persons and of all they possess in whatsoever way is in accord with
his most holy will.

22. Presupposition

That both the giver and the maker of the Spiritual Exercises may
be of greater help and benefit to each other, it should be presup-
posed that every good Christian ought to be more eager to put a
good interpretation on a neighbor's statement than to condemn it.
Further, if one cannot interpret it favorably, one should ask how the
other means it. If that meaning is wrong, one should correct the
person with love; and if this is not enough, one should search out
every appropriate means through which, by understanding the
statement in a good way, it may be saved.

23. Principle and Foundation

Human beings are created to praise, reverence, and serve God our
Lord, and by means of doing this to save their souls.

The other things on the face of the earth are created for the human beings, to help them in the pursuit of the end for which they are created.

From this it follows that we ought to use these things to the extent that they help us toward our end, and free ourselves from them to the extent that they hinder us from it.

To attain this it is necessary to make ourselves indifferent to all created things, in regard to everything which is left to our free will and is not forbidden. Consequently, on our own part we ought not to seek health rather than sickness, wealth rather than poverty, honor rather than dishonor, a long life rather than a short one, and so on in all other matters.

Rather, we ought to desire and choose only that which is more conducive to the end for which we are created.

230. Contemplation to Attain Love

Note. Two preliminary observations should be made.

First, Love ought to manifest itself more by deeds than by words.

231. Second, Love consists in a mutual communication between the two persons. That is, the one who loves gives and communicates to the beloved what he or she has, or a part of what one has or can have; and the beloved in return does the same to the lover. Thus, if the one has knowledge, one gives it to the other who does not; and similarly in regard to honors or riches. Each shares with the other.

The usual Preparatory Prayer.

232. *The First Prelude.* A composition. Here it is to see myself as standing before God our Lord, and also before the angels and saints, who are interceding for me.

233. *The Second Prelude* is to ask for what I desire. Here it will be to ask for interior knowledge of all the great good I have received, in order that, stirred to profound gratitude, I may become able to love and serve the Divine Majesty in all things.

234. *The First Point.* I will call back in to my memory the gifts I have received—my creation, redemption, and other gifts particular to myself. I will ponder with deep affection how much God our Lord has done for me, and how much he has given me of what he possesses, and consequently how he, the same Lord, desires to give me even his very self, in accordance with his divine design.

Then I will reflect on myself, and consider what I on my part ought in all reason and justice to offer and give to the Divine Majesty, namely, all my possessions, and myself along with them. I will speak as one making an offering with deep affection, and say:

"Take, Lord, and receive all my liberty, my memory, my understanding, and all my will—all that I have and possess. You, Lord, have given all that to me. I now give it back to you, O Lord. All of it is yours. Dispose of it according to your will. Give me love of yourself along with your grace, for that is enough for me."

235. *The Second Point.* I will consider how God dwells in creatures; in the elements, giving them existence; in the plants, giving them life; in the animals, giving them sensation; in human beings, giving them intelligence; and finally, how in this way he dwells also in myself, giving me existence, life, sensation, and intelligence; and even further, making me his temple, since I am created as a likeness and image of the Divine Majesty. Then once again I will reflect on myself, in the manner described in the first point, or in any other way I feel to be better. This same procedure will be used in each of the following points.

236. *The Third Point.* I will consider how God labors and works for me in all the creatures on the face of the earth; that is, he acts in the manner of one who is laboring. For example, he is working in the heavens, elements, plants, fruits, cattle, and all the rest—giving them their existence, conserving them, concurring with their vegetative and sensitive activities, and so forth. Then I will reflect on myself.

237. *The Fourth Point.* I will consider how all good things and gifts descend from above; for example, my limited power from the Supreme and Infinite Power above; and so of justice, goodness, piety, mercy, and so forth—just as the rays come down from the sun, or the rains from their source. Then I will finish by reflecting on myself, as has been explained. I will conclude with a colloquy and an Our Father.

From *The Constitutions of the Society of Jesus*

The six qualities treated in this chapter are the most important, and all the rest are reduced to them. For they include the general's perfection in relation to God; further, what perfects his heart, understanding, and execution; and further still, those qualities of body and those extrinsic goods which help him. Moreover, the importance of these six qualities is indicated by the order in which they are placed.

In regard to the qualities which are desirable in the superior general, the first is that he should be closely united with God our Lord and intimate with Him in prayer and all his actions, that from God, the foundation of all good, the general may so much the better obtain for the whole body of the Society a large share of His gifts and graces, and also great power and efficacy for all the means which will be used for the help of souls.

The second quality is that he should be a person whose example in the practice of all virtues is a help to the other members of the Society. Charity should be especially resplendent in him, toward all his fellow [human beings] and above all toward the members of the Society; and genuine humility too should shine forth, that these characteristics may make him highly loveable to God our Lord and to [all persons].

He ought also to be independent of all passions, by his keeping them controlled and mortified, so that in his interior they may not disturb the judgment of his intellect and in his exterior he may be so composed, particularly so self-controlled when speaking, that no one, whether a member of the Society who should regard him as a mirror and model, or an extern, may observe in him any thing or word which does not edify him.

However, he should know how to mingle rectitude and necessary severity with kindness and gentleness to such an extent that he neither allows himself to swerve from what he judges to be more pleasing to God our Lord nor ceases to have proper sympathy for his sons. Thus although they are being reprimanded or punished, they will recognize that in what he does he is proceeding rightly in our Lord and with charity, even though it is against their liking according to the lower man.

Magnanimity and fortitude of soul are likewise highly necessary for him to bear the weaknesses of many, to initiate great undertakings in the service of God our Lord, and to persevere in them with constancy when it is called for, without losing courage in the face of the contradictions (even though they come from persons of high rank and power) and without allowing himself to be moved by their entreaties or threats from what reason and the divine service require. He should be superior to all eventualities, without letting himself be exalted by those which succeed or depressed by those which go poorly, being altogether ready to receive death, if necessary, for the good of the Society in the service of Jesus Christ, God and our Lord.

The third quality is that he ought to be endowed with great understanding and judgment, in order that this talent may not fail him either in the speculative or the practical matters which may arise. And although learning is highly necessary for one who will have so many learned men in his charge, still more necessary is prudence along with experience in spiritual and interior matters, that he may be able to discern the various spirits and to give counsel and remedies to so many who will have spiritual necessities.

He also needs discretion in exterior matters and a manner of handling such diverse affairs as well as of conversing with such various persons from within and without the Society.

The fourth quality, one highly necessary for the execution of business, is that he should be vigilant and solicitous to undertake enterprises as well as energetic in carrying them through to their completion and perfection, rather than careless and remiss in such a way that he leaves them begun but not finished.

The fifth quality has reference to the body. In regard to health, appearance, and age, on the one hand account should be taken of propriety and prestige, and on the other hand of the physical energies which his charge requires, that in it he may be able to fulfill his office to the glory of God our Lord.

Thus it seems that he ought to be neither very old, since such a one is generally not fit for the labors and cares of such a charge, nor very young, since a young man generally lacks the proper prestige and experience.

The sixth quality pertains to extrinsic endowments. Among these, preference ought to be given to those which help more toward edification and the service of God in such a charge. Examples are generally found in reputation, high esteem, and whatever else aids toward prestige with those within and without.

Nobility, wealth which was possessed in the world, reputation, and the like, are extrinsic endowments. Other things being equal, these are worthy of some consideration; but even if they are lacking, there are other things more important which could suffice for election.

Finally, he ought to be one of those who are most outstanding in every virtue, most deserving in the Society, and known as such for a considerable time. If any of the aforementioned qualities should be wanting, there should at least be no lack of great probity and of love for the Society, nor of good judgment accompanied by sound learning. For in regard to other things, the aids which he will have (and which will be treated below) could through God's help and favor supply to a great extent for many deficiencies.[4]

Mary Ward (1585–1645)

Born of English Catholic nobility in 1585, Mary Ward grew up among Elizabethan gentry in a world where acts of Parliament had made it treasonous to be a Catholic priest or to hold the Catholic faith. Catholics, wealthy or poor, were persecuted, driven into hiding, imprisoned, and put to death. Mary received an unusually thorough Renaissance education from her grandmother and from Jesuit priests who lived in hiding in her home. At seventeen she resisted her family's attempts to arrange a marriage. Her reluctant father arranged her passage to St. Omer in Belgium where Mary founded a Poor Clare monastery for English noblewomen and began her own novitiate. Shortly afterward she experienced a call to establish an apostolic community of women like the Jesuits "only excepted which God by diversity of sex hath prohibited."[1]

Related by blood or marriage to most of the leading Catholics left in England, Mary attracted daughters and women servants of these families to join her. Taking a cue from Jesuit formation, the English Ladies secured a thorough education in theology, mathematics, classical languages, the arts, rhetoric, literature, and drama. The order grew rapidly and opened schools across the continent for girls and young women, teaching them not only to read, write, and guide a household, but to run small businesses, nurse the sick, provide spiritual direction and catechesis, care for the mentally ill, and comfort the brokenhearted. In their native England these women also disguised themselves as maids, housekeepers, widows, and craft makers to move through the households of both commoners and nobility, going where priests could not in order to draw lapsed Catholics back to the practice of their faith. Despite the success of the English Ladies' schools and missionary projects neither European civil society nor the Catholic Church was prepared for women to take such an active role in the service of faith or development of culture outside the home or cloister.

After years of growing ecclesial animosity, the church's German Inquisition imprisoned Mary Ward during the coldest months of 1630 although they pressed no formal charges nor held a formal trial. She was treated as a heretic without any evidence that she had ever said or written anything contrary to church teaching. Even after her release at Easter neither the ecclesial nor civil authorities brought formal charges against her. Nevertheless, Pope Urban VIII harshly suppressed the community of over a thousand women serving throughout Europe. Some of the group managed to stay together in small clusters of laywomen until they were reconstituted as a religious community some years later. Mary and some of her most loyal companions returned to England and lived in prayerful anonymity while her health failed. She died at the end of January 1645 and on her gravestone was inscribed: "To love the poor, persevere in the same, live, die and rise with them was all the aim of Mary Ward who having lived 60 years and 8 days died the 20 of January 1645."

Mary's collection of writings is not as familiar as that of Ignatius, but women called to the Ignatian spiritual path have long regarded her as an important voice of the tradition. Various scholars have gathered, collected, translated, and commented upon her journals, retreat notes, letters, and instructions to her sisters, along with the formula for her institute. Included here are short excerpts that illustrate the patiently discerning character of her spirituality and the centrality of God's will to her life. Despite great deprivation, both material and spiritual, Mary demonstrates humor, courage, humility, and the spiritual freedom she possessed to suffer rather than betray what she believed God was asking of her.

Among the writings of Mary Ward, "The Formula of the Institute" represents the foundational document for her apostolic order. The language of this document bears some resemblance to the Jesuit formula, but encapsulates the distinctive charisms the Spirit bestows on Ward and her followers.

Ward's "Instructions to Her Sisters at St. Omer" includes excerpts from a series of instructive talks she gave her novices during November 1617. In all ways she wanted the women of the community to be exemplars of "verity,"[2] the truth and justice of God embodied in a deep and abiding charity. What she terms "preceding" grace[3] is the a priori love of God that comes before humans perceive or understand their need for that love. This grace makes all goodness in humans possible. In scholastic terminology it is termed "actual grace."

We have included several excerpts from "The Letters of Mary Ward." There are 132 letters or fragments of letters of Mary still extant, although Mary wrote many more that were confiscated at the time of the suppression of her order in 1631. The first is typical of the many administrative letters she wrote to bishops, cardinals, and popes trying to secure ecclesial confirmation of her order and her rule. The church never granted such approval during her lifetime. Other fragments of letters come from the "lemon juice letters," so called because she wrote them on scraps of paper with lemon juice (referred to as liquor) while imprisoned in an unheated sickroom in a Poor Clare monastery outside of Munich. Having lived under persecution in England, Mary and her community leaders, Elizabeth Cotton and Mary Poyntz, knew how to carry on this secret correspondence. The text could only be seen or deciphered when the scraps of paper were held close to a fire. Unable to see or communicate with her, the sisters hid fresh lemons in the laundry and sewing packets, which they delivered several times a week. For fear of discovery, the texts of the letters were often in a kind of code. One lay sister, Anne Turner, remained with her in imprisonment.

Eileen Burke-Sullivan

From "The Formula of the Institute" in *Till God Will*

1. Whoever wishes to serve beneath the banner of the Cross as a soldier of God in our Society [. . .] should keep in mind the following: after a solemn vow of perpetual chastity, poverty and obedience, she is a member of a Society founded primarily for this purpose: to strive for the defence and propagation of the faith and for the progress of souls in Christian life and doctrine.

2. She will do this by leading them back from heresy and evil ways to the faith, to a Christian manner of life and to special obedience to the Holy See, assembling people and preparing them to attend public sermons and lectures; by performing any service of the word of God, by instructing girls in spiritual practices and simple people in Christian doctrine . . . by encouraging them to go to confession and to the other sacraments, preparing them for their reception. She will also see that preachers and spiritual fathers are sent to cities and to remote places, seek out women of doubtful lives and prepare them to receive the grace of the sacraments. . . . She will also help in reconciling those estranged from the Church, assist and serve prisoners and those in hospitals, in fact, undertake

any work of charity which seems proper to further the glory of God and the common good, yet altogether *gratis* and without receiving any stipend for these labours. [. . .]

4. . . . We pledge ourselves by a special vow to carry out whatever the present and future Roman Pontiffs may order which pertains to the progress of souls and the propagation of the faith; and to go without subterfuge or excuse, as far as in us lies, to whatsoever provinces they may choose to send us—whether they are pleased to send us among the Turks or any other infidels, even to those who live in the region called the Indies. [. . .]

6. No one should be admitted to profession in this Society without long and careful testing of her life and doctrine, as will be explained in the Constitutions. For all truth this way of life requires persons who are thoroughly humble and prudent in Christ as well as conspicuous in the purity of Christian life and learning.[4]

From "Instructions to Her Sisters at St. Omer" in *Till God Will*

While Mr. Sackville was commending us and our course and telling how much it was esteemed by men of judgment among the cardinals at Rome, Father Minister, who was present, answered: "It is true—while they are in their first fervour, but fervour will decay and when all is done, they are but women."

I would know what you all think he meant by this speech of his "but women," and what fervour is. Fervour is a will to do well, that is, a [preceding] grace of God and a gift given freely by God, which we could not merit. It is true that fervour doth many times grow cold, but what is the cause? Is it because we are women? No, but because we are imperfect women. There is no such difference between men and women.

Therefore, it is not because we are women but, as I said before, because we are imperfect women and love not [truth] but seek after lies. "*Veritas Domnini manet in aeternum*": the [truth] of the Lord remains forever. It is not *veritas hominum*, the [truth] of men, nor the [truth] of women, but *veritas Domini*, and this [truth] women may have as well as men. If we fail, it is for want of this [truth], but not because we are women.

Some religious, both men and women, have lost their fervour, because they have been unmindful of this [preceding] truth which is a gift of God; they have adhered to the sweetness they have found in prayer, and the content which they felt in the service of God. For all in the beginning do forsake the world for God only, which is [truth]. But, as I say, asking too much sweetness and feelings, which when they fail them and are left in aridity, God seeming to leave them, they think that they have lost their fervour. This is also a lie, since they may have fervour in aridity, fervour not being placed in the feelings but in a will to do well, which women may have as well as men.

There is no such difference between men and women; yet women, may they not do great matters, as we have seen by example of many saints who have done great things? And I hope in God it will be seen that women in time will do much.

This is [truth]: to do what we have to do well. Many think it is nothing to do ordinary things. But for us it is. To do ordinary things well, to keep our Constitutions, and all other things that be ordinary in every office or employment whatsoever it be. To do it well: this is for us, and this by God's grace will maintain fervour.

Heretofore we have been told by men we must believe. It is true, we must, but let us be wise and know what we are to believe and what not, and not to be made to think we can do nothing. If women are so inferior to men in all things, why are they not exempted in all things as they are in some? . . .

I would to God that all men understood this [truth], that women, if they will, may be perfect, and if they would not make us believe we can do nothing and that we are "but women", we might do great matters.

There was a Father that came recently to England, whom I heard say that he would not for a thousand worlds be a woman, because he thought that a woman could not apprehend God! I answered nothing but only smiled, although I could have answered him by the experience I have of the contrary.[5]

From "The Letters of Mary Ward" in *Till God Will*

To Bishop Albergati in Germany, 1620

This quiet lasted many weeks, until on St. Athanasius day, while sitting at work with the rest, there came suddenly on me such alteration and disposition that the operation of an unexpressible power could only cause, and certainty that there I was not to remain, that some other thing was to be done by me, but what in particular was not shown. The change and alteration this wrought for half an hour or more was extraordinary. I saw that this was to be so as if I had seen or heard it spoken.

To leave what I loved much and enjoyed with such sensible contentment, to expose myself to new labours, which then I saw to be very many; to incur the several censures of men, and the great oppositions which on all sides would happen, afflicted me greatly. Yet had I no power to will or wish otherwise than to expose myself to all these inconveniences, and put myself into God's hands with these uncertainties. By the advice of my confessor I continued the practice of that austere life half a year longer, the better to discover from whence that light came. When the rest were clothed, I departed from them, my confessor telling me I might be saved either by going or staying, which was all the encouragement or assistance any alive gave me at that time. . . .

My purposed time of stay in England expired, I returned to St Omer, with others who intended to be religious with me; great insistence was made by various spiritual and learned men that we would take upon us some rule already confirmed. Several Rules were procured by our friends both from Italy and France, and earnestly urged to make choice of some of them. They seemed not that which God would have done. And the refusal of them all caused much persecution, and all the more because I denied all and could not say what in particular I desired or found myself called unto. . . .

About this time, in the year 1611, I fell sick in great extremity, and being somewhat recovered and having made a vow to go in pilgrimage to Our Lady of Sichem, when I was alone and in some extraordinary repose of mind, I heard distinctly, not by sound of voice, but intellectually understood, these words: "Take the same of the Society." This I understood as that we were to take the same both in matter and manner, that only excepted which God by diversity of sex hath prohibited. These few words gave so great a measure of light in that particular Institute, so much comfort and strength, and so changed the whole soul that it was impossible for me to doubt but that they came from him whose words are works.

February 13, 1631

I had yours the last night. Lest I forget, I have little or no liquor left. . . . For my health, I am worse indeed, that is, my appetite is less, my nightly fever much greater, my catarrh and cough also more, but with all this and what else God will send, you and I must and will be most contented, till our Lord dispose otherwise. . . .

Propose to the Abbess as coming from yourselves that she should persuade me to drink some little thing in the morning, and the like in the afternoons, since I seldom eat bread or flesh, only taking liquids, as a little wine warmed with an egg, which Anne can do in my chamber; so please send me a couple of eggs every afternoon, for that afternoon and the next morning.

. . . we can only read once a day what you write because we lack fire. Your last papers I cannot warm till night.

The Lady Abbess is full of my writings: she has been in some hope that I might enter here, since my first vows, she tells me, were in St Clare's Order, but I pretend not to understand. . . .

[. . .] I think I am in a Cloister, and shut in. We are in one pretty little room on the first floor, joining upon the cemetery where they bury their deceased saints. Our habitation is the place of the despaired of sick. It seems that we have displaced one who is about to die any moment. She has been sick these past three years, and has spit up all her lungs. Here we sometimes fry and sometimes we freeze, and that's all there is to do. Three little windows closely walled up, our door chained and double-locked, and never opened but only at the entrance and departure of our two keepers, and the Lady Abbess who is the Chief Keeper. We were conducted here by the three who came with us and two Poor Clares who speak Italian.

Beds were placed by the door for the four nuns who guard us night and day. Mass and the Sacraments are not feasts for us to frequent, and for all this the place we inhabit has everything in it that could be wished for; indeed I say here and marvel at it, but our Lord and Master is also our Father and gives no more than is ladylike and is most easy to be borne. Be sure no complaints be made, nor notice taken of these things.

February 15, 1631

[. . .] For my being sent to Rome, if so it happen it will be perchance the best for us. But for the adverse part, I see not what it can profit them. For if they intend to have my life, they can kill me with less noise here; for in these parts they know no home nor friends. But here, or there, if God would have me die, I would not live: it is but to pay the rent a little before the day,[6] and to live and suffer for God, or to die and to go to him are both singular goods and such as I merit not, and one of the two, I trust, in the mercies of God will fall to my happy lot. . . . But I would have you both not the least troubled, but beg hard that he himself would do what he himself would have done.

February 18, 1631

I am heartily sorry for Father Ludovico. Let every one of the novices say a *Dirige* [a psalm from the beginning of Matins in the Office for the Dead] for his soul. I doubt he will not go alone, yet I am daily earnest with God in my poor manner that he would entirely pardon all our enemies, and let them go without further punishing them. It is good pleasing the Friend of friends and labouring in eternal works, and above all to be entirely and for ever at our Master's disposal.[7]

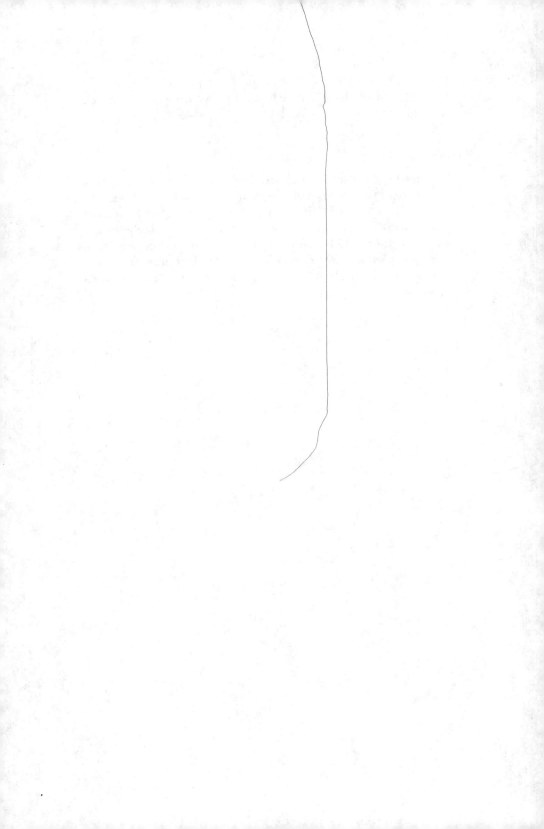

PART II
CONTEMPLATION IN ACTION

Two years after Ignatius' death, Pope Paul IV required that the Society of Jesus begin chanting the Divine Office in common as other religious orders customarily did. A decade later, Pope Pius V renewed the command and also required Jesuit scholastics to profess final vows before they were ordained to the priesthood. Both popes failed to appreciate the genius behind this new way of living the Christian Gospel and instead acted on the basis of a more traditional view of vowed religious life. In the classic monastic tradition work was undertaken as a means of practically supporting a life given to hours of liturgical prayer. Ignatian contemplation in action, by contrast, involves highly targeted prayer that supports the work of bringing forth God's reign in the ordinary routine of the world. Ignatian spirituality thus equips Christians to live their faith in the context of modern and now postmodern sensibilities.

It fell to Jerome Nadal, Ignatius' personal assistant, and Pierre Favre, one of the first companions, to defend by life and writing the unique features of this emerging tradition. Drawing on gospel images, the *Spiritual Exercises* encourages prayer that is rational, affective, imaginative, and practical. Those formed in this prayer tradition seek to discover God's will in the context of action rather than monastic silence. This explains the importance Ignatius gave to the examen, a brief prayer aimed at assessing one's heart to recognize patterns of desire that arise from God or contrarily from baser sources. As Nadal explains, the examen anchors a rhythm of daily prayer in which one achieves radical self-awareness in the midst of various tests. Likewise, Nadal coined the phrase "contemplatives in action" to capture the essence of the new way of life: Ignatius and his followers were given a particular grace to discover God's presence within the dynamic events of history that they were helping to shape.

Eileen Burke-Sullivan

25

Jerome Nadal (1507–1580)

Born in Majorca, Spain, in 1507, Jerome Nadal attended the University of Alcalá and there first became acquainted with Ignatius Loyola whom he thought to be too devout. He later moved to Paris to finish his studies for the priesthood and again met and occasionally associated with Ignatius' companions, but they could not persuade him to make the Exercises. Nadal was intellectually brilliant and determined to be a successful cleric, but Ignatius and his companions frightened him with their spiritual intensity that was politically dangerous in a climate that criminalized spiritual excess. It was nearly ten years later, after his ordination and first assignment in a wealthy parish on his home island of Majorca that he learned of the successful foundation of the Society of Jesus and its approval by the Catholic Church authorities. He journeyed to Rome to seek out his former classmates and discover the secret of their success. There he first made the Spiritual Exercises.

During the process of the retreat Nadal elected to join the Jesuits and he asked Ignatius to accept him as a novice. The father general had long recognized Nadal's intellectual gifts; he also valued his skills in administration and organization. In 1545, Nadal entered the novitiate and Ignatius assumed personal responsibility for his initial formation, as he had for his first companions. In consequence of this relationship it was Nadal who first recognized that the constitutive graces of the Jesuit vocation were the very graces that shaped Ignatius' own life.

After completing his early formation and professing his first vows, Nadal became a valued assistant to Ignatius who regularly empowered Nadal to represent his intentions and expectations for the different provinces in the Society. Like Pierre Favre, Nadal traveled all over Europe, to "expound to Jesuits the meaning of their institute and to enkindle their loyalty to it."[1] Indeed, both before and after Ignatius' death, it was Nadal who was most often sent to interpret and implement the *Constitutions* and occasionally respond to crises within the order.

Nadal was also responsible for developing a plan of studies that was to become the foundation for the *Ratio Studiorum*, the formal pattern for organizing education that all Jesuit schools followed until the suppression of the Society in 1773. As a student at the University of Paris, Nadal, like Ignatius, completely absorbed the Parisian model of education. Under Nadal's programmatic development and tutelage, the Jesuits imported this same educational model to China, India, the Americas as well as all the countries of Europe. Nadal died in 1580, twenty-four years after Ignatius. He thus lived to see the Society of Jesus spread all across the globe, firmly shaped by the *Spiritual Exercises* and the *Constitutions* that Ignatius wrote and that he himself helped implement.

Both an artist and a Scripture scholar, Nadal studied Hebrew with various Jewish scholars while completing a doctorate in Sacred Scripture at Avignon before joining the Society. In his last few years, he returned to this first love and published a book of scriptural meditations applying the Ignatian method of meditation to a series of original woodcuts that he created. Entitled *Observations and Meditations on the Gospels which are Read at Mass*, this collection has been reprinted numerous times in the ensuing centuries. In addition, his writings include instructions and commentaries on the *Constitutions*, obedience, Jesuit prayer, and many other topics written in his own hand in Spanish, Portuguese, or Latin.[2] He also delivered a number of sermons and instructions that were recorded by his assistants. Finally, his written corpus includes a memoir of Ignatius, Scripture commentaries, several catechisms, and a directory for giving the Spiritual Exercises.

Among the selections from Nadal's writings gathered here, *Instructions on Prayer* includes selected passages from his exhortations to the scholastics at Alcalá, Spain, given between 1553 and 1555 while he was promulgating the *Constitutions*. He gave similar instructions in other Jesuit houses.

Nadal's letter to Charles Borromeo reflects on the distinctive character of Ignatian spirituality as expressed in the Institute of the Society of Jesus. Bishop Borromeo had been assigned by Pope Gregory XIII to determine if the Jesuits should be exempted from singing the Office and allowed to bring their new members to vows after ordination to the priesthood. Nadal carefully explains to the papal representative his understanding of how Jesuit spiritual practice incorporates both contemplative and active dimensions and why Jesuit priests wait until after ordination before professing final vows. Borromeo was convinced by Nadal's argument and subsequently convinced Gregory to accept the order's unique practices.

"Any Other Ministrations Whatsoever of the Word of God" is an exhortation that Nadal probably wrote between 1573 and 1576. In the full exhortation Nadal examines the various ministries of the Society in light of the wisdom and teaching of St. Ignatius. This selection highlights the Ignatian tradition of spiritual conversation—a practice of the care of persons whereby one reaches out through warm and friendly conversation to awaken in another person a desire for the Christ life.

"Summary and Reminder" is a short spiritual memorial written to Gundisalvo Vaz, the Jesuit provincial of Portugal following Nadal's official visitation in 1561. It summarizes beautifully Nadal's practical approach to the life of contemplation in action, a life embodied first of all in the biography and practice of his spiritual mentor and friend, Ignatius.

Eileen Burke-Sullivan

From *Instructions on Prayer*

The Society pursues and embraces prayer by the grace of Jesus Christ. It teaches prayer first and foremost through its Spiritual Exercises, to which we see that God our Lord has given such effectiveness, to the greater glory and praise of his divine majesty. The Exercises have the greater spiritual effectiveness in our Lord the greater the humility and the less the curiosity, the greater the faith and trust that the Lord will act through them, the greater the desire for the salvation and perfection of our own souls, the greater the application and exactness, and the greater the desire for the glory and praise of Jesus Christ, with which we make them. What in our Lord is of most avail in the Exercises and in all prayer is a great generosity in surrendering to God all our powers and operations, and all that we are; and also, while not failing with his grace to do our part by every virtue and means to perfection, to hope constantly, desire intensely, and beg from God that he might bring about in them and in all whatever will be for his own greater glory and praise. . . .

Thus it is characteristic of the Society's prayer that it extends to the practice of vocal prayer and every exercise of the Society's ministries; and that, so far as can be attained by the grace of Jesus Christ, the enlightenment of the understanding and the good affection of the will and union persist in, accompany, and guide all our operations, so that in all things God our Lord is found. . . . In this way prayer should be so directed that by its extension it augments and guides and gives spiritual relish to one's works, along with strength in the Lord, and so that the works will enhance prayer, giving it power and joy. In this way, Martha and Mary being joined together and assisting one another, not just a part of the Christian life is embraced. . . .

Prayer can be made from all created things: in them beholding, praising, and loving their Creator, Preserver, and Ruler, etc. . . . and, inasmuch as prayer is a gift of God our Lord, a living spiritually, a mystical understanding of things spiritual and of God, and a finding God our Lord in every thing and every action, each one according to the measure of God's grace given him and his own cooperation with it in great humility, simplicity, purity of heart, faith and hope in God our Lord, being all afire with the fervor of charity and zeal for God's honor and glory in the salvation of souls—whoever practices prayer will easily find matter for meditation and every kind of prayer in the Lord. . . .

It helps to know that there are two ways of moving into prayer. One is by simple and humble meditation on created things, another is, by a previous inspiration of grace with some higher illumination, to reach the point of considering and contemplating God in everything below him, in that light gently seeking greater deployment of the divine power in greater and clearer truths. In addition there is another even higher way: when God gives a very lofty grace and light in which the supreme truths are contemplated in a unity (felt by those who experience this) and with that illumination they look at and contemplate everything else in the Lord. . . . We must take special care to be devoted to the Exercises and let ourselves be led by them, for they are the starting-point from which Father Master Ignatius came to such high contemplation and prayer and to God's being able to achieve such great effects through him. . . .

Each should strive to carry over the Society's prayer and contemplation to the ministries he performs, which are all spiritual: preaching, expounding Scripture, teaching Christian doctrine, giving the Exercises, hearing confessions, administering Holy Communion, and attending to other good works. In these ministries they should find God with peace, tranquility, and application of the inner person; with light, joy, satisfaction, and warmth of charity for God. And thus they should seek the same in all other ministries, even exterior ones.[3]

From a Letter to Charles Cardinal Borromeo in *Walking in the Spirit*

Wherefore, ours is not a monastic order, nor should it be judged in terms of other orders of clerics with a rule, but according to its own end and the means necessary for that end.

Hence the Society is substantially and of its very Institute a religious order that is contemplative as well as active.

We practice the contemplative life in meditation, prayer, and in the diligent and ongoing use of all the spiritual exercises. For, without the spiritual vitality that prayer preserves, the Society could not practice the active life with proper dignity. . . .

Wherefore, the Society as a religious order is multiplex, as if to say many religious orders rolled into one through the divine goodness. For the Society was instituted for contemplation, for preaching and hearing confessions, for other spiritual ministries, for the corporal works of mercy, and finally for study: for the teaching of theologians is that religious orders can be instituted for all these purposes.

For these reasons (that our way of living is so broad, or ministries so multiple, so difficult, and so exhausting), it follows that our times of probation, or novitiate, should be very lengthy and carefully done, our obedience most demanding, and every aspect of the religious life perfect as far as possible. Then also, since we have so many difficult and necessary occupations—mind you—lest souls be lost for whom Christ Jesus was crucified and died, we judge that certain rituals are not proper for us since they can impede our ministries, just as certain things are suitable for other religious orders and other things are not. Besides, we also take care that those to be professed have not only been proved in the practice of living after the manner of religious, but have also been sufficiently trained in the ministries that they have to undertake. Whence it follows that they should first be priests before they are professed. Other religious orders train their novices in choir and in other ceremonies; we train ours in the ministries proper to our Institute, those that prepare our men to undertake those ministries of the Society for the salvation of souls.[4]

From "Any Other Ministrations Whatsoever of the Word of God" in *The Conversational Word of God*

It is a great grace in the Church of God, and a high office, to be a minister of God's word; and this is a thing we should try to grasp with heart and mind, brethren. . . .

But what are those aspects of the ministry of the word that we have treated up to now only implicitly?

The first aspect is private spiritual conversation, which is an excellent method of helping our neighbor. . . .

Pierre Favre, one of the first companions of Ignatius, was one of those apostles who had a special talent in this ministry. He had an extraordinary charm in spiritual conversation, for Pierre Favre never met a man, no matter how far gone, who was not totally changed by dealing with him. Father Ignatius used to say that Pierre could draw water from a rock. . . .

It is the special quality of the conversational apostle quietly and slowly to win over his neighbor, to deal with him gently and light the flame of charity in his heart. . . .

[Ignatius] taught not only by word, but also by example. The first thing to do is to concentrate one's heart and soul in loving the person you want to aid. Even though the person in question was a hardened sinner, he found something in him to love, his natural gifts, his belief in God, and any other good things about him. . . .

One should watch carefully for an occasion to give the conversation a religious turn. Father Ignatius used to speak of this method as "entering by their door so as to come out by our door.". . . After chatting about politics and news, we should move onto . . . the life of Christ, his teachings and death.[5]

From "Summary and Reminder" in *The Jesuits: Their Spiritual Doctrine and Practice*

Do all for the greater glory of God. Love the Institute. Love the end [of the Society]. Love and desire to work for that end. Perfect obedience. Prayer which is practical and carried into execution (*practica y extendida a la obra*). Simplicity. Love of mortification. Love of suffering. Modesty in speech coupled with edification. Love to be despised. Diligence in daily observances. Walk before God and always in His presence. Practice the acts of the theological virtues, especially of charity. Develop the habit of an ever-activated love of

God, in such a manner that this love may always be the motivating force in all one's actions, and that it may be the form of all the virtues and give them the superior value of charity.[6]

Pierre Favre (1506–1546)

Pierre Favre was one of Ignatius' earliest and most faithful companions. Born on April 13, 1506, to a farming family in Savoy, France, Favre manifested both intellectual promise and a kind of precocious orientation to holiness when he was a child. He determined to study for the priesthood and his local pastor, an unusually well-educated man, tutored him in Latin and in the general studies he would need to begin studies at the College of St. Barbe at the University of Paris. There, along with Francis Xavier, Favre shared a room with Ignatius for over six years.

Ignatius was nearly fifteen years older than his roommates, but they were ahead of him in their studies toward a master of theology degree and ordination to the priesthood. Favre tutored Ignatius in theology while Ignatius, aware of the younger man's various spiritual crises, became the guide of his soul. Ignatius helped Favre discover interior peace, a growing confidence in his priestly vocation and, eventually, a call to be his companion in the founding of the Society of Jesus.

Of the many companions that Ignatius attracted through his years of study in Spain and later Paris, Favre was the first to truly "throw in his lot" with Ignatius and become his lifelong companion. Favre was also the first to be ordained a priest. Thus, he presided at the Eucharist in the chapel on Montmartre during which the small group of seven men professed their vows together in August of 1534. Ignatius delayed nearly five years before directing Favre in the Spiritual Exercises, however, because he could see that the young Savoyard suffered deeply from religious scruples that rendered him doubtful that God could forgive him and love him unconditionally. When Favre finally received the grace of the Principle and Foundation, however, he was so deeply imbued with the knowledge of God's love that he later became the most expert spiritual director of all the early companions according to Ignatius (who included himself in the comparison).

Favre's ministry in the Society was mobile. Between 1539 and 1546 two different popes directly missioned him to a variety of tasks in cities of Italy, Germany, France, and Spain. He traveled mostly on foot, carrying only a few possessions. He was often hungry, cold, exhausted, and subject to robbery or harassment by soldiers. In each place where he was sent he undertook the work of spiritual direction and the giving of the Spiritual Exercises. He preached, taught catechism, heard confessions, and sought ways to reconcile various Protestant leaders with the Catholic Church. He laid the groundwork for new Jesuit foundations and he served as a theological expert for a number of bishops and archbishops preparing for the Council of Trent.

Favre is the model of Ignatian disponability—the quality of being available to be sent wherever his superiors determined the most urgent and necessary work to be done would be best accomplished by him. Even more than Ignatius, who was firmly settled in the work of directing the new order from Rome, Favre lived as a pilgrim, constantly on the road with "nowhere to rest his head" (Luke 9:58). On August 1, 1546, worn out from his extensive travels and from a chronic fever, Favre died in Rome. His death triggered an outpouring of grief among all who knew him. Years later Simão Rodrigues, another of the first companions, wrote about Favre: "In his dealings with others he revealed such a rare and delightful sweetness and charm as I have never to this day, I must admit, found in anyone else. In some way or other, he used to make friends with people, and by the kindness of his manner and speech so won his way into all hearts that he set them on fire with the love of God."[1]

The selections presented here include four brief passages from Favre's spiritual journal, *The Memoriale of Pierre Favre*.[2] Favre, perhaps more than any other of the first companions, discovered that this tool facilitated his contemplation and helped him discern the presence of God's direction in his very active life. We have also included excerpts from *The Letters of Pierre Favre*. Here one finds detailed recommendations for the spiritual life, reports on his work, and answers to theological questions put to him by one or another of his correspondents. We also find in his letters the indications of loving companionship that endeared him to others and made his ministry remarkably effective. Favre's profound respect for those he served, and those he served with, is made evident in the way he not only wrote to his correspondents in their languages; he also signed his own name according to the language of the one he was writing to. Favre's unfailing generosity and compassion—even while dying—is evident in his last letter, written to Laínez just a week before he died.

Eileen Burke-Sullivan

From *The* Memoriale *of Pierre Favre* in *The Spiritual Writings of Pierre Favre*

January 6, 1545

On the day of the Three Kings in the year 1545, I thought of the following subject to preach on: If Jesus Christ wished, among other things, to be hidden behind the veil of his flesh, it was to teach men to reveal their dispositions towards him. For the same reason he willed to conceal under his flesh all the treasures of divine knowledge so as to give us an opportunity of dispensing the treasures we have received from his Majesty. And he acted in such a way that the three Magi and all their servants opened up their treasures when they saw the poverty of their Lord. In short, while concealing his greatness, he brings his angels down to earth to proclaim it; while concealing his sinlessness and wishing to be baptized by John, he moves the Father to make it known in these words: "This is my beloved Son . . ." [Matt. 3:17]. Again, while not wishing to manifest his charity at the wedding feast, he opens up the treasures of his mother when she says to him, "They have no wine" [John 2:3], thus constraining him to manifest his glory before the time.

Today the Church celebrates these three manifestations. . . .

Then I experienced some kind of obstinate resistance in my soul which prevented me from delighting in the joy and fervor attached to a feast so sacred and sublime. I received this interior reply about it: "This is the day of the Three Kings, the day the true King is adored. Therefore, bear the burden of that resistance in the knowledge that thereby you will more clearly see whether you are king over yourself or not. It is a small thing to master and conquer ourselves when we find ourselves near to Christ by devotion. But the true victory, the true mastery and control of oneself, can be better recognized when our King seems no longer present—he who wages our wars for us until he makes kings of us in the end" [1 Sam. 8:20].

February 20, 1545

On the Friday after Ash Wednesday, I experienced a great desire that our Society should not lose anything by using the new Roman Breviary.

I feared the usual consequences: that Ours might make ill use of the privilege by which they are not bound to recite numerous long offices aloud. So I celebrated Mass for this intention, namely, that through the offices of working and of prayer of the heart, we may fully compensate the living and the dead for our making less of the vocal office. This will be easy for those who love God and their neighbors; for, by preaching, hearing confessions, and personal exhortation together with mental prayer, they can help both the living and the dead, making known to many of the faithful the needs of the dead and keeping their memory alive among themselves.

But if we do not see this, it will be preferable for us to be bound to a longer office and have less time available for other pious activities and prayers. In short, no one should waste time.

Let us help the living in all their needs, spiritual first, then corporal. Let us help the dead by engraving their needs deeply on our memories and by inducing others, penitents, congregations, those we meet and converse with, to do the same. And let us form many to take our place and recite the offices we are unable to say ourselves.

April 30, 1545

On the last day of April, the birthday of St. Catherine of Siena, I celebrated Mass for the successful outcome of the so anxiously awaited Council of Trent. I found a special formulary for that intention in the rite of the church of Valladolid. The petitions in it were that the Lord deign to provide for his Church through this council.

There came to my mind the needs of sinners, who will more easily be converted if the ministers of God's word and of the sacraments are reformed first; likewise the needs of all the afflicted, who will very much benefit when charity, now growing cold, recovers its vigor. There before me appeared the sick, for example, as if expecting assistance; and, on the other hand, the dead whose holy yearnings now come to naught appeared to me as if in exceeding torment at the thought that the heirs to their property and the ministers of the Church were not carrying out their duties in a fitting manner.

In this way many other benefits to be provided for by the council occurred to me so that I might desire them.

May 8, 1545

On the day of the Apparition of St. Michael the Archangel, I arrived at Madrid to visit some noblemen and some friends in Christ. I had come from Valladolid, and during the journey I thought of many ways of instructing an old man who belonged to the group called *romeros* in Spanish [pilgrims who have gotten a bad name because of misdeeds on pilgrimage]. I was also given an opportunity of consoling a greatly afflicted woman who had opened her whole soul to me. While staying in inns, I have always felt inspired to do good by instructing and encouraging people.

In the eyes of Christ and of his heavenly court, it is very good to leave in the inns and houses where we happen to stay some trace of good and holy behavior; for everywhere there is good to be done, everywhere there is something to be planted or harvested. For we are indebted to all men in every condition and in every place, just as we are looked after and strengthened everywhere by our most high Lord, whose fellow workers we are.[3]

From *Selected Letters and Instructions of Pierre Favre* in *The Spiritual Writings of Pierre Favre*

To the Sodality at Parma, September 7, 1540

Since I must depart from Parma for Spain, I wanted to satisfy the excellent desire expressed by you and many other persons like you, who would not remain content with me unless I left them a remembrance, not of my person, but of the procedure they ought to follow in the way of God when they have no other instructor.

First, I would not have you mistakenly think that for your perseverance I would give you a different food from what I have given you hitherto. The philosopher would tell you the same: speaking of bodily food, he says that the same things which nourish a person also enable him to grow. Hence, you must stoutly believe that the spiritual exercises in which you have found nourishment for your spirit up to the present will still be necessary for you in the future, your essential food having been above all the heavenly bread on which the angels and all the saints always have been and always will be fed. This bread is far more important for your spiritual life than material bread is for your temporal life. Similarly for the other spiritual exercises: self-examination, confession, meditation, prayer, and the works of mercy.

You must be convinced that if by means of these exercises you have obtained some knowledge of yourselves and abnegation, some love of God and neighbor, it will be necessary in the future as well to continue steadily in these excellent practices with greater fervor of spirit. . . .

[Whether] before the crucifix or at Mass listen to some word or think of some action of Christ in which to mirror yourselves and arouse yourselves to live well, not only that day but always and forever, grieving always for your sins and longing to live a better life. . . .

Never fail to go to confession and Communion at least once a week. Your other spiritual practices—prayer and meditation—which you perform daily, you should order to one or all of the following three effects: the honor of the Lord God and of his saints, your own salvation, and the salvation of your neighbors both living and dead. In this way, you will be growing daily through these devotions in some virtue that is needed for the better performance of your actions: humility, patience, prudence, and the like; you will grow in the knowledge and love of God; you will grow in love for your neighbor. Thus you will be able to stride forward on the way of salvation, ordering your spiritual life step by step. . . .

Your brother and spiritual father in Christ Jesus,
Don Pietro Fabro

To the Jesuits at Coimbra, Portugal, March 2, 1545

The grace of Our Lord Jesus Christ and the charity of the Holy Spirit be always in your hearts. . . .

So this is where I send you, dearest brothers, as I say fare you well: to the one whose saying farewell makes us fare well indeed, and whose making us fare well confers true welfare—him to whom I would also have prayers arise that your blessing might be of his dew and his fatness [see Gen. 27:28], for there is no other fullness in any creature of which you can all receive [see John 1:16]. May your smell be like that of the plentiful field which was blessed by the Lord

Jesus [see Gen. 27:27]. (I here speak of the blessing which I know you want me chiefly to ask for you.) May these blessings come upon you and overtake you. May you be blessed in the field of the Lord, and blessed among the citizens of the heavenly Jerusalem. Blessed be the fruit of your wombs, the fruit of your lips and works; blessed be the barns of your minds and blessed be your stores; blessed be your goings in to your own interior selves and your goings out. May your enemies fall down before your face; if they come out against you one way, may they flee before you seven ways. May the Lord send a blessing upon the storehouses of your three interior powers, and upon all the works of your hands. May he bless you in the institute to which you have bound yourselves, and may he raise you up as a holy congregation for himself. May the Lord open his excellent treasure, the heavens, that he may give your earth spiritual rain in due season. May the Lord and his kingdom be above you, so that your minds may be drawn upwards; may he be within you, so that you may be truly rooted in him; may he be as a firm foundation beneath you, so that you may always rely upon him; may he be at your right side, so that he will never let you swerve to pleasures or vanities; may he be at your left, so that you may never be broken by adversity; may he be behind you, so that through fear of him you will be recalled from any backsliding onwards to your perfection.

But let this be enough. May God do all this, whose spoken blessing effects the good it contains. . . .

You most loving brother in Christ,
Petrus Fabri

To Diego Laínez from Madrid, March 7, 1546

Dearest Brother in Jesus Christ:

May the grace and peace of our redeemer be always in our souls.

I never replied to the request you made in several letters that I send some guidelines for those who wish to save souls among the heretics and help their own. I may fairly claim your pardon, both because I lacked time to think about the matter and because there was no leisure here in the house. At present I might excuse myself by saying that my hand is not as strong as it ought to be—although the best excuse would be to acknowledge that nothing occurs to me that would be pertinent to your query. However, I shall say a few things that have lately come to me.

1. Anyone wanting to help the heretics of this age must be careful to have great charity for them and to love them in truth, banishing from his soul all considerations which would tend to chill his esteem for them.

2. We need to win their goodwill, so that they will love us and accord us a good place in their hearts. This can be done by speaking familiarly with them about matters we both share in common and avoiding any debate in which one side tries to put down the other. We must establish communion in what unites us before doing so in what might evince differences of opinion.

3. Inasmuch as this sect of Lutherans are "children of withdrawal unto perdition" [Heb. 10:39] who lost the true attitude of heart before losing the true faith, we have to proceed with them from what helps toward the true attitude of heart to what helps toward true faith. It is just the opposite with the entrance of neophytes into the faith: the latter must first have their minds taught and corrected by means of the faith that comes from hearing, and then move on to the proper attitude of heart regarding moral teaching and works in accord with the faith they have received.

4. When undertaking to deal with a person not only of evil and corrupted doctrine but also of evil life, we must first find roundabout ways to dissuade and remove him from his vices before speaking to him about his errors of belief. . . .

7. A man who can speak with them on how to live well, on the virtues and on prayer, on death, judgment, hell, and the like—matters that lead even a pagan to amendment of life—will do them more good than another who is filled with theological authorities for confounding them.

8. In sum, these people need admonitions, exhortations, and the like, on morals, fear and love of God, and good works, to counter their weaknesses, want of devotion, dissipations, anxieties, and other evils; the latter are not mainly or even originally a matter of the mind but of the hands and feet of the soul and body. . . .

Pedro Fabro

To Diego Laínez from Rome, July 23, 1546

Dearest brother in Christ: . . .

I do not know whether you have received word of the bodily death of your father according to the flesh. I learned of it through a letter from your sister Doña María. I sent her a reply to console those left behind in this life: your lady mother, your two sisters, and little Cristóbal. Be sure to write them yourself about this for their consolation—and do so all the more fully the further removed your own spirit is from being upset or inordinately disconsolate. To recommend his soul to you it will suffice for you to reflect upon what a son like yourself owes to a father such as yours (may he be in glory). I had the Masses said here by the fathers in the house, as well as earlier in Spain, writing, if I remember rightly, to Portugal, Valladolid, Alcalá, Valencia, and Barcelona, besides what I did while passing through various places where there are people who grieve at events of this sort, which are rightly a source of sorrow to the whole Society and to all who are close to it. But do not let this keep you from also fulfilling your own filial duty in this regard by writing to the dispersed brethren personally. . . .

Your brother in the Lord,
Pedro Fabro[4]

PART III
MISSION

A spirit of apostolic mission permeates the Ignatian vision. The twentieth-century French historian of spirituality, Joseph de Guibert, asserts that it is the most important principle of Ignatian spirituality. Broadly speaking, mission is understood to be service of the Gospel, according to God's will and plan, by one who is sent. (The English word "mission" derives from the Latin verb *mitere*, "to send.") The Gospel of John portrays Jesus as sent by the Father to accomplish the salvation of the world (John 3:16-17; 20:21). Likewise, Jesus' followers confidently believe that he has sent them to cooperate with the Spirit in bringing God's reign to realization "on earth, as it is in heaven." This same spirit of mission pervades the *Spiritual Exercises* of St. Ignatius. The Second Week begins with the famous "Call of the Earthly King," where the one making the Exercises imagines Jesus issuing an invitation to join him in his mission to win the whole world for God. The remaining Exercises follow the basic logic of the gospels and invite the one making them to accompany Jesus as a disciple on mission.

Shortly after the founding of the Society of Jesus a new type of missionary impulse exploded in the church, impelled in part by Christian Europe's global expansion and led by the followers of Ignatius—among them the great patron of the missions, St. Francis Xavier. This explosion, unlike anything seen since the earliest days of the church, sprang from the heart of the Ignatian charism and, not surprisingly, was interpreted as an almost literal continuation of the apostolic journeys fifteen hundred years earlier. Part 3 of *The Ignatian Tradition* presents three chapters that sketch the lives and select from the writings of three early Jesuit missionaries to Asia and the Americas: Xavier, Roberto de Nobili, and Antonio Ruiz de Montoya.

Eileen Burke-Sullivan

43

Francis Xavier (1506–1552)

Francis Xavier, a Basque nobleman, scholar, and priest, set sail from the port of Lisbon, Portugal, on an arduous eight-thousand-mile ocean voyage on his thirty-fifth birthday in April of 1541. He departed, at the command of Pope Paul III, to bring the Gospel to the peoples of what are today India, Indonesia, and all the lands of Eastern Asia. Francis never returned to Europe. He never again saw the beloved faces of his friends and companions with whom he had lived for seven years, while completing his theological studies at the University of Paris. He left behind a comfortable life as a pastor or bishop in his native Spain and took up the task of becoming one of the greatest missionaries in Christian history.

Born Francisco Jassu Azpilcueta de Xavier on April 7, 1506, into both Basque and Spanish nobility, Francis was the youngest of five children, and the one destined by parental ambition and family need to take up theological education with an eye to an appointment as a bishop or an abbot with substantial status and financial support. At nineteen, Francis left the Xavier home for the University of Paris where he met and took up residence with a fellow theology student named Pierre Favre in the College of Saint Barbe. Sharing the same birth year, a similar sharp intelligence, and a mutual interest in theology the two rather quickly moved to a deep friendship. In 1529 Ignatius of Loyola came to live with the younger men as they pursued together the master of arts degree in theology at the college. Xavier excelled at sports and in the classroom, but he was driven by his family's ambition for the wealth and status of a benefice. Over time, however, his companionship with Ignatius and Favre, his participation in the Spiritual Exercises, and the grace of God transformed his worldly ambition into the evangelical desire of "helping souls," an ambition that played out on a worldwide stage.

Francis was the first of many members of the fledgling Society of Jesus to respond to a papal appointment outside of Europe. In fact, it is to Xavier, even more than Ignatius, that the phenomenal growth of the order in its early days can be credited. Xavier's letters to the members of the Society generated enormous enthusiasm for the work of proclaiming the Christian faith in these distant parts of the world, and ignited the desire to serve the Gospel in the hearts of thousands of missionary successors through the succeeding four and a half centuries.

Xavier served as papal nuncio of India and other Asian lands, as superior to the mission to India, and eventually as provincial of the new province of India. Throughout this time he engaged in the direct works of evangelizing, baptizing, and catechizing new believers. His one unfulfilled hope was to get to China, but he became fatally ill and died in a Portuguese enclave on Shangchuan Island, off the coast of China, on December 3, 1552. He and Ignatius were canonized together in 1622.

Xavier's preserved writings include a substantial volume of public letters to the order recording the work of the mission and the need for additional help. They also include numerous personal letters to his family, to Ignatius, Favre, and other close friends among the companions. In addition, he wrote small catechisms and prayer books in various languages for the instruction of the Portuguese, Indian, Indonesian, and Japanese Christians he evangelized and catechized. The selections presented below all come from his letters addressed to his companions in Europe after he left on his lifelong missionary voyage. These brief passages capture his sense of profound unity with Ignatius and the other companions, his disponability to God's will, and his total commitment to the third degree of humility in service of the standard of Christ.

Eileen Burke-Sullivan

From *The Letters and Instructions of Francis Xavier*

To Companions in Rome, January 15, 1544

During this time there were so many who came and asked me to come to their homes to recite some prayers over their sick, and others who came in search of me because of their infirmities, that the mere reading of the Gospels, the teaching of the boys, baptizing, translating the prayers, answering their questions, which were never failing, and then the burial of the dead left me no time for other occupations. . . .

I could never come to an end in describing to you the fruit that is being gained by baptizing newborn children and teaching those who are old enough to learn. . . .

Many fail to become Christians in these regions because they have no one who is concerned with such pious and holy matters. Many times I am seized with the thought of going to the schools in your lands and of crying out there, like a man who has lost his mind, and especially at the University of Paris, telling those in the Sorbonne who have a greater regard for learning than desire to prepare themselves to produce fruit with it: "How many souls fail to go to glory and go instead to hell through their neglect!"[1] And thus, as they make progress in their studies, if they would study the accounting which God our Lord will demand of them and of the talent which has been given to them, many of them would be greatly moved, and taking means and making spiritual exercises to know the will of God within their soul, they would say, conforming themselves to it rather than to their own inclinations: *"Lord here I am! What would you have me do? Send me wherever you will, and if need be, even to the Indies!"*

I fear that many who study in the universities study more to obtain honors, benefices, or bishoprics with their learning than with the desire of adapting themselves to the demands of these honors and ecclesiastical states. . . . [Yet] how many millions of pagans would become Christians if there were laborers . . . *persons who seek not what is their own but what is of Jesus Christ* (Phil 2.21).

May 10, 1546, To Companions in Europe

For the love of Christ our Lord and of his most blessed Mother and of all the saints who are in the glory of paradise, I ask you, my dearest Brothers and Fathers, that you be particularly mindful of me and continuously commend me to God, since I live in such great need of his favor and assistance. I have great need of your continual spiritual assistance, for from much experience I have come to know that God our Lord has, through your intercession, helped and assisted me in many toils of body and spirit. So that I may never forget you and ever have a special remembrance of you, I would have you know, dearest brothers, that for my own consolation I have cut your names from the letters which you have written to me with your own hands so that I may constantly carry them with me together with the vow of profession which I made because of the consolations which I received from them. I give thanks first of all to God our

Lord, and then to you, most dear Brothers and Fathers, for the fact that God has so made you that I derive such great consolation from bearing your names. And since we shall soon see each other in the next life with greater peace than we have in this, I say no more.

Your least brother and son,
Franciscus.

To Ignatius, January 29, 1552

May the grace and love of Christ our Lord ever help and assist us. Amen.

My true Father: I recently received a letter from your Holy Charity in Malacca when I was returning from Japan; and God our Lord knows how much my soul was consoled on receiving news of your life and health, which I cherish so highly. And among the many other very saintly words and consolations which I read in your letter were these last, which said "Entirely yours, without my being able to forget you at any time, Ignatius;" and, just as I then read them with tears, so I am now writing these with tears, as [I] recall times past and the great love which you ever had, and still have, for me; and as I also reflect upon the many toils and dangers of Japan from which God our Lord freed me through the intercession of your Charity's holy prayers.

I would never be able to describe the great debt that I owe to the people of Japan, since God our Lord, through respect for them, gave me a great knowledge of my infinite iniquities; for, being apart from myself, I did not recognize the many evils that were within me until I saw myself amidst the toils and dangers of Japan. God our Lord made me clearly feel the great need which I had of one who would take great care of me. Your Holy Charity may now see the burden that you are giving me in the care of so many holy souls of the Society who are here, since I clearly know, apart from the mercy of God, my great inadequacy in this regard. I was hoping that you would commend me to those of the Society and not them to me.

Your Holy Charity has written to me that you have a great desire to see me before you leave this life. God our Lord knows what an impression these words of great love made upon my soul, and how many tears they have cost me whenever I recall them; and it seems to me that I shall have this consolation, since nothing is impossible to holy obedience.

Least son and farthest exile,
Francisco.[2]

Roberto de Nobili (1577–1656)

In the generation following Xavier numerous Jesuits traveled to Eastern Asia, including Matteo Ricci (1552–1610), a mathematician and scientist who learned Mandarin, translated numerous Western scientific texts into Chinese, and studied Confucianism and Buddhism in order to successfully proclaim the Christian message in this utterly new world. Another Jesuit to follow in the footsteps of Xavier, spending most of his life in India, was Roberto de Nobili. Like Ricci, this scion of one of the oldest Roman noble families was gifted with an extraordinary intelligence, a facility for languages, and an appreciation of culture. Formed in the Ignatian principle of finding God in all things, he was able to recognize the work of God's Spirit in completely new cultural settings and adapt the Christian message using non-European categories.

When de Nobili came into contact with the ironbound caste system of India, he perceived that the Gospel would never penetrate that vast population without appealing to the Brahmins. This in turn could only happen if he came to them as a philosopher they could trust. His understanding of the mindset of wealthy, educated, and powerful elites helped him to adapt his Western ways to the Indian culture. He adopted the dress, customs, rigid diet, and behavior of a Hindu Brahmin ascetic. He mastered Sanskrit and Tamil, and finally won the admiration and friendship of a competent Brahmin teacher who guided him through the philosophical thicket that provided the basis for Hindu thought. Through the next forty years he wrote over twenty volumes of Catholic teaching in Sanskrit and Tamil. Out of the Christian scholastic tradition, he addressed with special care the particular questions for which Hindu philosophers were most eager to find answers. His ability to appeal to all kinds of people allowed de Nobili to win converts from every strata of society.

In 1615, at the suggestion of the Archbishop of Cranganore, India, de Nobili composed a report for Fr. Claudio Aquaviva, the general of the Society of Jesus. He titled it *Concerning Certain Customs of the Indian Nation* and divided it into eleven chapters that describe certain Indian customs in detail. He carefully analyzes the social implications and possible religious (and thereby possibly superstitious) implications of these customs. The last part of the report included here summarizes the principles of adaptation that de Nobili worked under.

In *The Dialogue on Eternal Life* de Nobili adopts the classical literary form of a dialogue. A "master" responds to the philosophical and theological queries of a "disciple" in language and categories that make sense to the disciple. Thus, de Nobili presents Thomistic theology and philosophy, as well as Ignatian spiritual insight, in the entirely new context of south Indian religious thought. The term "Veda" is defined by de Nobili earlier in the text as referring either to divine revelation itself or to a specific text of that revelation.

Eileen Burke-Sullivan

From "Concerning Certain Customs of the Indian Nation" in *Preaching Wisdom to the Wise*

It is of the very nature of truth that the more closely it is examined with all fidelity and sympathy, the more splendidly does it shine forth and the more firmly grounded it proves itself to be in the eyes of judicious investigators. Working on this principle and with no other end in view than the glory of God and the salvation of souls, during the last three years [1610–1613] I have been examining anew and with perseverance revolving in my mind the truth of those statements which bear on the customs of this country. . . .

In furthering the conversion of souls and in the matter of adopting or allowing the customs of the unbelievers, the preacher of Christ should always comport himself in such a manner as to preclude anything that is in the least sinful, even were he thereby to secure the conversion of the whole world. He should weigh with all care and discernment which of these customs are purely social, and which are tainted by superstition. Otherwise, it may well happen that in eagerly pursuing the good of creatures, he may betray both the grace of the Creator and the salvation of his own soul, and (as happens not infrequently) ultimately render unstable and altogether unprofitable the very spiritual fruit he expected for the neighbor. But as perfectly true as this principle is, we should beware of that other rule which some people seem to prescribe in deciding matters of custom prevalent among the people here. That rule goes to the other extreme and sins by excessive scrupulosity; it is so radical that, to judge by the common talk, its imposition would entail for these people not only the denial of the very necessities of life, but also the forfeiture of everything. Such an extreme policy (I should think) would find little favor with him who made himself all things to all men that he might win them all the Christ, and who, far from condemning offhand the various customs of the peoples he evangelized, made himself, as it were, a man outside the law for the sake of those who were outside the law.[1]

From "The Dialogue on Eternal Life" in *Preaching Wisdom to the Wise*

Disciple: You are explaining these characteristics so that we can discern the truth; why must the person who listens be without bias and without inordinate attachment to anything?

Master: If not, the mind would not be able to grasp the truth, even if one were to hear it in an ordinary and normal way. To a sick person whose tongue is affected by a preponderance of bile, sweet things like sugarcane, etc., taste bitter. Similarly, when the mind is biased towards falsehood and obstinately remains unduly attached to it, even if it hears the truth it dislikes it and does not accept the taste of truth. If sugarcane tastes bitter, it is the fault of the mouth, not of the sugarcane. So too, if the truth appears different and without its real taste to a mind affected by sickness and addicted to falsehood, this is a flaw in the mind; one cannot conclude that it is a fault in the flawless truth. That is why we said that one who is desirous of seeking the truth must be free from undue attachment to things.

To write a correct letter in the place of a wrong letter written on a palm leaf, one must first delete the wrong letter and then write the correct one. The mind is like the writing tablet; if a falsehood has been written there like an incorrect letter, it is not proper to imprint the truth, which is like a correct letter, without first eradicating the falsehood by scraping it off. This is why we say that one desirous of knowing truth must be like a palm leaf with nothing written on it, possessing a mind untainted by inordinate attachments to anything.

Disciple: What you have said is indeed reasonable. . . . As you have required above, my mind is longing for truth; it is without bias and I have given up all inordinate attachments. So kindly teach me the truth which you see fit to impart to me.

Master: To discern which Veda comes from the Lord and which is not from him is difficult for people whose minds are deluded by sin, biased in favor of falsehood, and inordinately attached to things. But it will be easy for those who eagerly search for truth and are untainted by sin. To such people the merciful Lord will make known his Veda by one means or another, in some way or another, and they will accept it with the Lord's help as soon as they hear it.

The first characteristic of the Lord's Veda is that it must appear to the mind as reasonable, since it is entirely true. The mind will perceive and accept it with full consent, since it is in accordance with the mind. Light should be acceptable to the healthy eye, not unpleasant. Similarly, the truth, which is like a light, should be acceptable to the healthy mind devoid of sin, not otherwise. . . .

That is why the Veda revealed by the Lord . . . is like a good father to the mind. Like a good teacher the Lord will teach the truth that is agreeable to the mind, including hidden truths. The mind will escape the anxiety of not seeing the truth and will rest content in full acceptance. It will be free from doubt and remain firm in the truth.

Disciple: Kindly tell me why the mind so completely accepts this religious viewpoint that contradicts reason, and thus does not reach the satisfactory state proper to itself.

Master: They establish their viewpoint by arguing that apart from what is seen nothing else exists. They do not accept inference and scripture in addition to direct perception. But there cannot be any lie more blatant than what they say. . . . Why then cannot one look at the great house of the world and say that there is someone who built it? Seeing a flood in the river, one can say that a cause exists for the flood, even if this cause is not seen. The world is like the river; when one sees so many things come into being in a proper way, remain [for a time] and then disappear, how can one deny the existence of the cause, even if one does not see it? . . .

Moreover, even if by faulty thinking the followers of this viewpoint deny that verbal knowledge is a proper means of knowledge, they should eventually accept it. How can anyone know that he was born to his father, or that his mother bore him in her womb? He has not seen this for himself. But one can know by inference that just as there are fathers and mothers for others, he too must have a father and a mother. But inference does not show that he was born to this particular father or that this particular mother gave him birth. Therefore, he trusts the words of other people in the world and says "This one is my father," and "That one is my mother." One therefore has to admit that scripture is means of knowledge beyond direct perception and inference. If one can accept in faith what is said by human beings who are less intelligent and who tell lies at various times for various reasons, how much more would it be against reason and logic not to accept in faith what was revealed by the Lord, who is infinite knowledge himself and who is by essence true? The Lord is the cause of the world, by nature he is all good, and he is the protector of all people.

Therefore, intelligent people cannot think that the Lord would not give the Veda so that they could follow righteousness and avoid sin. In regard to many other things, people trust the testimony of the world and believe that many things which they have not seen exist. So why cannot the testimony of all people be accepted when people say, "The Lord exists"? When one accepts the truth that the Lord exists, this becomes a great shining light to all people.[2]

Antonio Ruiz de Montoya (1585–1652)

While Xavier, Ricci, de Nobili, and their companions were preaching the Gospel to ancient civilizations in Eastern Asia, other followers of Ignatius left Europe to work on the continents of North and South America. Here the colonizers found civilizations that ranged from the great empires of the Aztecs, Incas, and Mayas, to relatively small tribal groups of indigenous peoples inhabiting vast prairies and dense jungles. Once the Aztec and Incan empires fell, the conquistadores moved with alarming speed to conquer and control the Americas and enslave its native inhabitants. In both North and South America missionaries faced the task of presenting the Christian faith in widely varying situations, among many languages, and with differing levels of receptivity. They also inherited the terrible challenge of protecting the indigenous peoples from the depredations of their fellow Europeans. But just as the missionaries to Asia were scholars in secular disciplines and languages, so too were those who served in the Americas. Geography, cartography, biology, languages, medicine, and history were all fields of scholarship to which they contributed their expertise.

Most of the North American work of evangelization began more than a half-century after the first missions to South America. The Jesuits and some lay associates formed in Ignatian spirituality accompanied the French colonists to what is today the Maritime Provinces of Canada as early as 1604.[1] The dramatic work of the canonized North American martyrs, Jean de Brébeuf, Isaac Jogues, and their companions, of Jacques Marquette, who explored of the Mississippi River Valley, and of Pierre Jean De Smet, the nineteenth-century missionary to the tribes west of the Mississippi, have all been well chronicled. On the South American continent the level of scholarship and missionary contribution was every bit as extensive and dramatic, but the work was carried on quite differently. In the heart of the continent, in what today encompasses western Brazil, northern Argentina, and most of Paraguay, the Jesuits established their famous *reducciónes*, or "reductions."[2] The Jesuits designed these mission communities to protect hundreds of thousands of indigenous peoples and to bring to them both the Christian faith and European civilization. The Guariní people, for example, living in small groups under a *cacique*, or chieftain, proved ready prey for the European conquistadores who came with their guns and swords looking for lands and slaves.

In addition to proclaiming and practicing the Catholic faith in the context of stable, self-governing socio-political communities, the Jesuits established schools to rival the finest schools in Europe in the study of language, the arts, architecture, music, mathematics, cartography, medicine, law, theology, philosophy, and natural sciences. They handed on and continued to develop the newest information in farming and animal care as well as multiple skills of weaving, sewing, carpentry, stonework, tile making, sculpting, tool making, and printing. The people built printing presses, publishing works by native writers that were wildly popular in Europe. The Jesuits supported self-governance by the indigenous peoples and generally provided communication with the European kings, in order to maintain legal protections for the natives from the rest of the colonial population. The reductions lasted nearly two centuries until they were finally destroyed only after the Jesuits were driven out of Spain and Portugal and all their colonies in 1767.

Antonio Ruiz de Montoya became one of the more famous missionaries of the Paraguay reductions. Born in Lima, Peru, in 1585 to a wealthy Spanish captain and his Peruvian common-law wife, he was orphaned with wealth but minimal supervision as a young child. Out of a reckless adolescence he rather dramatically experienced a call to enter the Society of Jesus and eventually serve as a missionary to the native peoples of his own continent. At the request of his novice master he became proficient in the very difficult Guaraní language and was sent with an experienced missionary to what is today Cordoba, Argentina, to found a new Jesuit province.

In later years Antonio and his fellow missionaries described themselves as spiritual conquistadors, winning souls for Christ out of love and care for the natives' well-being and salvation. He served as a superior of the reductions for many years, and then was sent by his provincial to represent the cause of the Native Americans before the Spanish and Portuguese courts in Europe. In this work he served brilliantly and achieved all that the Jesuit leadership could hope for. While in Europe Antonio wrote an account of the founding and early years of the reductions called *The Spiritual Conquest*, which continues to be used by historians and geographers of South America as one of the most vivid and accurate descriptions of the daily life and struggles of the native peoples.[3]

As one of the earliest cartographers of South America, Ruiz de Montoya developed hundreds of detailed maps of the entire region. He wrote both a grammar and a dictionary of the Guaraní language; both are still cited today. He also wrote four mystical treatises that have been preserved in the official Jesuit archives in Rome. The stories of the spiritual, physical, and scholarly labor of the Jesuit and lay missionaries marvelously illuminate the concepts of *magis* and mission that are at the heart of Ignatian spirituality. Their writings further disclose these values in tandem with other Ignatian ways of thinking and acting.

Ruiz de Montoya's book on the reductions, *The Spiritual Conquest*, devotes several chapters to a crucial moment when, after more than fifty years of successful community life and education, nearly fourteen thousand Guaraní were forced to flee their long-established towns and lands. We gather excerpts from this story in "Solidarity with a People in Exodus." The Guaraní and the missionaries canoed down the Paraná River, negotiating by portage two massive waterfalls, while Portuguese slavers sought to capture them. They moved inland to an unoccupied area less accessible to those who sought to enslave them. The people suffered from hunger, disease, and a variety of natural dangers including drowning, poisonous snakes, wild animals, dangerous insects, and exhaustion. Ruiz de Montoya compares the journey to the Exodus account of the Israelites.

"The Power of the Gospel" comes from a later chapter of the same book. Here, Ruiz de Montoya explains to the Spanish king the spiritual and human success of the Jesuit missions. He defends the commitment of the missionaries' lives as well as their challenging work, describing in detail the reality of their situation while refuting the scurrilous charges propagated by rumor to undermine the Jesuits and their mission in South America. Along the way he gives a moving apology for his own commitment to his people, their history, and their plight.

Eileen Burke-Sullivan

Solidarity with a People in Exodus (From *The Spiritual Conquest*)

The town of São Paulo is situated in the south. It is the most inland settlement on the entire coast, sixteen leagues from the sea. It is protected by a towering mountain range called Paraná Piacaba, meaning a place from which one sees the sea. The mountains are so steep that four men could block the way of large armies. Easy access to the town might be afforded by a gradual road from the Janeiro River, if a section of the forest were opened up, but the people of São Paulo strongly resist this. It is quite fertile country; there are wheat, maize, wines, beef, and pork. These are raised there and carried for sale throughout the coast upon the backs of Indian men and women, who are forced to bear loads like mules even if they have children to raise. The inhabitants of the town are Castilians, Portuguese, Italians, and people of other nationalities gathered there by a desire to live as they like in freedom, without the constraints of law. Their way of life is destruction of the human race: they kill all those who flee from them to escape the wretched slavery they inflict upon them.

They go out for two or three years at a stretch hunting human beings like animals. Some have been out ten or twelve years. . . . These people, worse than brigands, invaded our reductions; they seized captives, killed, and pillaged altars. . . .

Father Francisco Vázquez Trujillo, then provincial superior, had visited the entire territory during this time. He was present at the destruction of San Javier. Grasping the situation clearly, he ordered us to arrange things in great secrecy, so that when it became necessary to move because of the common enemy we could do so safely and calmly. He undertook to get the [King's regent] in Chuquisaca to approve this.

The watch that we constantly maintained advised us that the enemy were on their way. At this the Indians determined to move— to abandon their lands in order to preserve their lives and their freedom. This move was facilitated by an official request from the authorities in the city of Guairá, who asked us to move the people because their own forces were too slight to help us against such an aggressive enemy. The request was utterly disingenuous and deceitful. The Spaniards planned to intercept us on the road and, like the men from São Paulo, steal our sheep [the native people] and divide them among themselves. Subsequent events showed this, although their plan failed. The move was also expedited by the fact that the Indians had already provided themselves with canoes, since their exit would have to be made down the Paraná.

It was an amazing sight, the entire shore filled with Indians busily building rafts—these were made by joining two canoes or two large logs dug out like boats, and placing on top a well-roofed cabin that gave good protection from rain and sun. The people were all busily carrying down to the shore their furnishings, stores, livestock, and birds. The noise of tools, the haste and confusion, all made clear that the day of doom was near. Who could think otherwise when they saw us six or seven priests consuming the Blessed Sacrament, taking down the religious pictures, consuming the oils, and gathering up the vestments; likewise disinterring the buried bodies of the three outstanding missioners so that, having been the companions of our travails, they might share this final one with us and not be abandoned in the wilderness; and leaving behind our lovely, beautifully decorated churches, which we closed up tight to keep them from becoming the lairs of beasts? . . .

When the time came for the exit of this nation of Israel, in flight like Jacob from a barbarous people, they sat on the banks of the river and recalled with emotion their present hardships, anxiety, and poverty, as they found themselves driven in flight from their own lands by persons who in justice should have been their protectors. With emotion they recalled their houses, and above all the house of God where for so many years they had worshiped, humbly served, and received him into their souls in the life-giving Sacrament. They still had the harps and musical instruments which they had used to make music to God in their homeland on festival days, their devotion swelling amid sweet motets and their prolonged sessions in church seeming short as they listened to the sound of their well-tuned instruments. Now stringless, broken, and serving but to bring back sad memories, these were abandoned among the crags of that rugged trail.[4]

The Power of the Gospel (From *The Spiritual Conquest*)

For a better understanding of the reductions mentioned earlier and those described below, I shall here set down a number of general remarks applicable to all the reductions and settlements. It is not my intention to speak of the virtues and achievements of the laborers in this vineyard, men who left their native countries, families, and comforts and penetrated into foreign lands, sacrificing themselves to hunger, nakedness, and even the sword (as we shall see), renouncing the acclaim they would have garnered here in Spain for their teaching, preaching, and other distinguished activities—lures that can bring down the highest-flying falcon. Nor do I wish to compare this spiritual conquest with other splendid ones. This conquest is completely lacking in outward splendor; it has only the interior splendor of countless souls. . . .

It is the power of the gospel that I seek to set forth. Its potency is manifested by gentling lions, taming tigers, transforming wild beasts into human beings and even angels. To give an idea of the toil and hardships of those who labor in this vineyard and create the towns—of which I shall make simple mention—would require rehearsing here [St. Paul's] litany of his hardships in the second letter to the Corinthians, which, while describing the saint's own experience, is equally valid today.

At this point I will review the various practices and customs which have been established by dint of our constant preaching, along with some other comments, so that I will not need to repeat them for each reduction. . . .

They all raise food, and each man has his own plot. When past eleven years of age boys have a plot of their own. Upon these they very cooperatively assist each other. They neither buy nor sell, for they freely and unselfishly help each other in their needs, and show great generosity to people passing through. Accordingly, there is no theft; they live in peace and without quarrels. . . .

Those who are qualified receive Communion four times annually, when they have a public festivity with a preparation by sermons and pious stories, fasts, disciplines, and other penances. Those who belong to the sodality of the Blessed Virgin, and some who do not, go to confession weekly; the less zealous every month. . . .

They are highly capable in mechanical matters. There are excellent carpenters, ironworkers, tailors, weavers, and shoemakers. Though they possessed none of these skills before, the systematic effort of the Fathers has made them masters of them, not least in effective cultivation of the earth with the plow. They are remarkably attached to the music in which the Fathers instruct the caciques' children, along with reading and writing. They celebrate Mass with elaborate music for two or three choirs. They play musical instruments with great skill: bassoons, cornets, oboes, harps, zithers, guitars, rebecks, clarinets, and other instruments. This greatly contributes to attracting pagans and making them eager to bring us into their lands to form and teach their children. . . .

They have erected hospitals for treating the poor, the men separate from the women. The Fathers have taught them how to bleed and frequently practice it themselves; they have appointed infirmarians who do their job diligently. They have other practices of this sort which give shape to an excellent civilized commonwealth. . . .

Many among the Spanish are eager for His Majesty to hand the Indians over to them in *encomienda* [i.e., forced labor] after the ten years of exemption granted them by His Majesty following the reception of baptism, thus to impose upon them the unparalleled yoke of personal service—the measure devised by Pharaoh for oppressing the people of Israel—which in the Indies has caused the death of countless people without hope even of eternal life because of their want of instruction, their continuous occupation (as His Majesty puts it in his royal letters patent) in this diabolical personal service denying them the time to acquire and practice it. Furthermore, these persons have attributed the issuance of the royal letters patent not to His Majesty's Christian zeal or to his obligation to protect a people destitute of all human protection, but rather to what they call the interfering obstinacy of the Society. In this way they turn this most Catholic measure of His Majesty to our discredit, endeavoring to persuade the high officials here at court that we exploit the Indians in Paraguay for our own profit. . . .

We would indeed deserve censure if we exposed ourselves to the frequent risk of death incurred in those parts for the sake of temporal interests. It would also be the height of imprudence to forsake the religious advantages of a college for the extreme stress of life among pagans if our purpose were any merely human interest. No sensible Christian will see anything wrong in our teaching the Indians how to farm so they can procure what they need to cover themselves (this is all the patrimony they can aspire to), lest nakedness be an excuse for not coming to church to hear God's word, as sometimes happens. Indeed, one ought to consider them bound to do this as shepherds of that flock.

I freely acknowledge that my objective is to preserve the Indians from personal service. My purpose herein is the common good of both Indians and Spaniards. The arguments for this are given by His Majesty in his royal letters patent which I shall place at the end. It is not my objective that they should be idle—that would be a blameworthy objective indeed. Rather, I desire that they pay His Majesty the tribute which their poverty allows, for they will have plenty of struggle to support themselves and their families. If His Majesty vouchsafes to use these tributes to reward the services rendered by Spaniards, it will be justly done and no one will object; indeed, we ask and petition that they be compensated with these tributes. But to place the Indians in their power—the personal service would furnish them a knife for butchering the sheep of Jesus Christ like the sheep in a slaughterhouse.[5]

PART IV
CITIZENSHIP AND PROPHECY

"Their minds are occupied with earthly things. But our citizenship is in heaven," St. Paul writes in his letter to the Philippians (3:19-20). Taken literally and out of context, this injunction might lead to extreme religious sectarianism where the sacred and profane never overlap. In contrast, Ignatian spirituality seeks God precisely in the world. It courageously engages worldly issues and affairs. It aims always for the *magis* but it does not for that reason shy away from controversy or conflict, from political, economic, or cultural concerns, from all that goes by the name "the secular." Rather, it seeks God precisely in the world, in the wide range of symbols and languages accessible to various peoples, realms, and regions of life and thought. As the Salvadoran theologian and martyr Ignacio Ellacuría tellingly argues, "to be committed only to the religious aspect of the Kingdom, without concern for its essential reference to the world and history, would be a clear betrayal of God's history; it would leave the field of history to God's enemies."[1]

From the perspective of Ignatian spirituality, therefore, "citizenship in heaven" finds a body in and through genuine citizenship in the world. Furthermore, genuine citizenship in the world requires a prophetic stance when worldly values conflict with the values of God's kingdom, when human injustice imprisons the truth (see Rom 1:18), when ideology, selfishness, and hatred threaten to turn God's world into a hell. Over and over the followers of Jesus, like Jesus himself, have paid the price of speaking the truth of God's kingdom in opposition to worldly power. The integration of prophecy and citizenship, while not unique to Ignatian spirituality, is central to it; the presence in history of many Ignatian martyrs, including the three Jesuits featured in these chapters, testifies to the importance of this integration.

Kevin F. Burke, s.j.

Edmund Campion (1540–1581)

Edmund Campion is perhaps the best known among the forty Roman Catholics who were martyred in England and Wales between 1535 and 1679 and canonized three centuries later by Pope Paul VI on October 25, 1970. He was born into a Catholic-turned-Anglican family in London the same year that Ignatius and his first companions founded the Society of Jesus. An outstanding scholar and orator, he attended St. John's College, Oxford. In fact, Campion made such an impression on Queen Elizabeth when she visited Oxford in 1566 that she wanted to take him into her court. Two years later he took the oath of supremacy and was ordained a deacon in the newly established Church of England. He seemed destined for worldly greatness, but shortly after his diaconate ordination he began experiencing unsettling doubts about his religious profession. In 1569, impelled by what he called "a remorse of conscience and detestation of mind," he left England and spent the next two years in Ireland. After much wrestling with God, with questions of religion, and with himself, he came back to London having rejoined the Catholic Church. Unable to stay in England, he journeyed to France and later to Rome where he joined the Society of Jesus in 1573 and was ordained a priest several years later.

In June, 1580, Everard Mercurian, the fourth superior general of the Society of Jesus, sent Campion, Robert Persons, and Ralph Emerson back to their native England to serve the persecuted Catholic community there. The Jesuits traveled and worked clandestinely; at that time to be or to harbor a Catholic priest in England was considered high treason, a crime punishable by death. Campion is known to have traveled among various towns from London to Berkshire, Oxfordshire, Lancashire, Yorkshire, and back again. He typically stayed in Catholic homes, usually for only one or two days at a time. In each place he visited he taught catechism, celebrated Eucharist, and heard confessions before moving on. He wrote several treatises and books while in England, including a Catholic apologetic entitled *Rationes decem* [*Ten Reasons*] and the selection included here known as "Campion's Brag." Thirteen months after he arrived in England, Campion was captured by a government spy, committed to the Tower of London, tortured, tried, convicted of treason, and, on December 1, 1581, brutally executed.

Written against the backdrop of the Elizabethan Age (1558–1603), "Campion's Brag" laces general elements of contemporary Catholic apologetic with specific elements drawn from Campion's Ignatian formation: a hunger to serve God's greater glory, indifference as to where he was sent, absolute obedience, total confidence in God. It was not Campion but his enemies who gave this selection (known more formally as "The Challenge to the Privy Council") its informal title. Campion, however, did supply grounds for calling it such: after protesting that he "would be loath to speak anything that might sound of any insolent brag or challenge," he indeed appears to boast, saying that "no one Protestant, nor all the Protestants living, nor any sect of our adversaries . . . can maintain their doctrine in disputation" against him. "Campion's Brag" is reproduced here in full.[1]

Kevin F. Burke, s.j.

"Campion's Brag"

To the Right Honourable, the Lords of Her Majesty's Privy Council:

Whereas I have come out of Germany and Bohemia, being sent by my superiors, and adventured myself into this noble realm, my dear country, for the glory of God and benefit of souls, I thought it like enough that, in this busy, watchful, and suspicious world, I should either sooner or later be intercepted and stopped of my course.

Wherefore, providing for all events, and uncertain what may become of me, when God shall haply deliver my body into durance, I supposed it needful to put this in writing in a readiness, desiring your good lordships to give it your reading, for to know my cause. This doing, I trust I shall ease you of some labour. For that which otherwise you must have sought for by practice of wit, I do now lay into your hands by plain confession. And to the intent that the whole matter may be conceived in order, and so the better both understood and remembered, I make thereof these nine points or articles, directly, truly and resolutely opening my full enterprise and purpose.

1. I confess that I am (albeit unworthy) a priest of the Catholic Church, and through the great mercy of God vowed now these eight years into the religion [religious order] of the Society of Jesus. Hereby I have taken upon me a special kind of warfare under the banner of obedience, and also resigned all my interest or possibility of wealth, honour, pleasure, and other worldly felicity.

2. At the voice of our General, which is to me a warrant from heaven and oracle of Christ, I took my voyage from Prague to Rome (where our General Father is always resident) and from Rome to England, as I might and would have done joyously into any part of Christendom or Heatheness, had I been thereto assigned.

3. My charge is, of free cost to preach the Gospel, to minister the Sacraments, to instruct the simple, to reform sinners, to confute errors—in brief, to cry alarm spiritual against foul vice and proud ignorance, wherewith many of my dear countrymen are abused.

4. I never had mind, and am strictly forbidden by our Father that sent me, to deal in any respect with matter of state or policy of this realm, as things which appertain not to my vocation, and from which I gladly restrain and sequester my thoughts.

5. I do ask, to the glory of God, with all humility, and under your correction, three sorts of indifferent and quiet audiences: the first, before your Honours, wherein I will discourse of religion, so far as it toucheth the common weal and your nobilities: the second, whereof I make more account, before the Doctors and Masters and chosen men of both universities, wherein I undertake to avow the faith of our Catholic Church by proofs innumerable—Scriptures, councils, Fathers, history, natural and moral reasons: the third, before the lawyers, spiritual and temporal, wherein I will justify the said faith by the common wisdom of the laws standing yet in force and practice.

6. I would be loath to speak anything that might sound of any insolent brag or challenge, especially being now as a dead man to this world and willing to put my head under every man's foot, and to kiss the ground they tread upon. Yet I have such courage in avouching the majesty of Jesus my King, and such affiance [trust] in his gracious favour, and such assurance in my quarrel, and my evidence so impregnable, and because I know perfectly that no one Protestant, nor all the Protestants living, nor any sect of our adver-

saries (howsoever they face men down in pulpits, and overrule us in their kingdom of grammarians and unlearned ears) can maintain their doctrine in disputation. I am to sue most humbly and instantly for combat with all and every of them, and the most principal that may be found: protesting that in this trial the better furnished they come, the better welcome they shall be.

7. And because it hath pleased God to enrich the Queen my Sovereign Lady with notable gifts of nature, learning, and princely education, I do verily trust that if her Highness would vouchsafe her royal person and good attention to such a conference as, in the second part of my fifth article I have motioned, or to a few sermons, which in her or your hearing I am to utter such manifest and fair light by good method and plain dealing may be cast upon these controversies, that possibly her zeal of truth and love of her people shall incline her noble Grace to disfavour some proceedings hurtful to the realm, and procure towards us oppressed more equity.

8. Moreover I doubt not but you, her Highness' Council, being of such wisdom and discreet in cases most important, when you shall have heard these questions of religion opened faithfully, which many times by our adversaries are huddled up and confounded, will see upon what substantial grounds our Catholic Faith is builded, how feeble that side is which by sway of the time prevaileth against us, and so at last for your own souls, and for many thousand souls that depend upon your government, will discountenance error when it is bewrayed [betrayed; divulged], and hearken to those who would spend the best blood in their bodies for your salvation. Many innocent hands are lifted up to heaven for you daily by those English students, whose posterity shall never die, which beyond seas, gathering virtue and sufficient knowledge for the purpose, are determined never to give you over, but either to win you heaven, or to die upon your pikes. And touching our Society, be it known to you that we have made a league—all the Jesuits in the world, whose succession and multitude must overreach all the practice of England—cheerfully to carry the cross you shall lay upon us, and never to despair your recovery, while we have a man left to enjoy your Tyburn, or to be racked with your torments, or consumed with your prisons. The expense is reckoned, the enterprise is begun; it is of God; it cannot be withstood. So the faith was planted: So it must be restored.

9. If these my offers be refused, and my endeavours can take no place, and I, having run thousands of miles to do you good, shall

be rewarded with rigour [severity], I have no more to say but to recommend your case and mine to Almighty God, the Searcher of Hearts, who send us his grace, and see us at accord before the day of payment, to the end we may at last be friends in heaven, when all injuries shall be forgotten.

Alfred Delp (1907–1945)

Alfred Delp was born in Mannheim, Germany, on September 15, 1907. The second oldest child in a family of six, his father was Lutheran and his mother a Roman Catholic. He was raised and deeply influenced by both traditions, but as an adolescent he became active in the Catholic parish in nearby Lampertheim. Following the completion of his classical German secondary studies in 1926 he joined the Jesuits. He traversed the latter stages of Jesuit formation during the frightening years of Hitler's rise to power and emerged with an Ignatian voice uniquely attuned to the great Christian theme of Advent. During his Jesuit regency—a period between philosophy and theology studies spent teaching high school—he wrote and produced a Christmas play entitled *The Eternal Advent*. A decade later, in the months before his death, he wrote a series of Advent meditations that are among his most profound writings.

In 1935, near the end of his first year of theological studies, Delp published *Tragic Existence*, an analysis of the philosophy of Martin Heidegger. After his ordination in 1937 and his tertianship (the final year of Jesuit formation) he planned to begin doctoral studies in social philosophy at the University of Munich. But as a sign of the times and a sign of things to come, his acceptance to the program was arbitrarily revoked by Nazi officials. This was not his first run-in with the Reich: Hitler had already closed the high school where Delp was teaching shortly after ascending to power. Yet it was an illuminating introduction to the arbitrary exercise of force, and ironically it contributed to his real education: he developed a passionate understanding of the political implications of the Gospel and the demands of genuine citizenship in the face of bald ideology.

For several years after his ordination Delp worked at the Jesuit periodical, *Stimmen der Zeit*. After the Gestapo shut the magazine down in 1941 he moved into parish ministry. His provincial, Augustin Rösch, fully aware of Delp's interest in political and social reality (not to mention his fierce opposition to the Nazi project) introduced him to a resistance group known as "the Kreisau Circle." An ecumenical group founded by Helmuth von Moltke with the express purpose of dreaming a new Germany beyond National Socialism, it included professionals, academics, army officers, and religious leaders. They met in various locations, among them, Delp's rectory. After the failed attempt on Hitler's life in 1944 and because several members of the Kreisau Circle were loosely connected to the attempted coup, the Gestapo arrested Delp after Mass on July 28, 1944. He was imprisoned on the specious charge that he helped plan the assassination attempt. Although acquitted on this charge he was found guilty of treason by virtue of his being a Jesuit. Alfred Delp was hanged in Plötzensee prison on February 2, 1945.

The collection of Alfred Delp's writings published posthumously under the title *The Prison Meditations of Father Delp* includes a variety of brief spiritual meditations, including the aforementioned Advent reflections, along with personal journal entries and letters written during the months of his imprisonment in the fall of 1944. Penned on scraps of paper that were hidden in his laundry, these writings were smuggled from the prison by two women friends. The first section here is his diary entry dated January 1, 1945, a month and one day before his execution. The second focuses on an Advent figure whose destiny resembled his own, Saint John the Baptist. The third selection is an excerpt from a longer reflection that combines elements of a diary entry and a general letter to friends and supporters. The final piece, the last of Delp's known writings, is his farewell letter to his brother Jesuits.

Kevin F. Burke, s.j.

From *Alfred Delp, s.j.: Prison Writings*

Jesus. The name of our Lord and of my Order shall be the first word I write in the New Year. The name stands for all the things I desire when I pray, believe and hope; for inner and outer redemption; for relaxation of all the selfish tensions and limitations I place in the way of the free dialogue with God, all the barriers to voluntary partnership and surrender without reserve: and for a speedy release from these horrible fetters. The whole situation is so palpably unjust;

things I have neither done nor even known about are keeping me here in prison.

The name Jesus stands also for all that I intended to do in the world, and still hope to do among humankind. To save, to stand by ready to give immediate help, to have goodwill toward all people, and to serve them, I still owe much to so many.

And in conclusion the Order, too, is embraced in my invocation of this name—the Order which has admitted me to its membership. May it be personified in me. I have pledged myself to Jesus as his loving comrade and blood-brother.

The Name stands for passionate faith, submission, selfless effort and service.[1]

The man crying in the wilderness. We live in an age that has every right to consider itself no wilderness. But woe to any age in which the voice crying in the wilderness can no longer be heard because the noises of everyday life drown it—or restrictions forbid it—or it is lost in the hurry and turmoil of "progress"—or simply stifled by authority, misled by fear and cowardice. Then the destructive weeds will spread so suddenly and rapidly that the word "wilderness" will recur to our minds willy-nilly. I believe we are no strangers to this discovery.

Yet for all this, where are the voices that should ring out in protest and accusation? There should never be any lack of prophets like John the Baptist in the kaleidoscope of life at any period; brave men and women inspired by the dynamic compulsion of the mission to which they are dedicated, true witnesses following the lead of their hearts and endowed with clear vision and unerring judgment. Such persons do not cry out for the sake of making a noise or the pleasure of hearing their own voices, or because they envy other people the good things which have not come their way on account of their singular attitude toward life. They are above envy and have a solace known only to those who have crossed both the inner and outer borders of existence. Such persons proclaim the message of healing and salvation. They warn us of our chance, because they can already feel the ground heaving beneath their feet, feel the beams cracking and the great mountains shuddering inwardly and the stars swinging in space. They cry out to us, urging us to save ourselves by a change of heart before the coming of the catastrophes threatening to overwhelm us.

Oh God, surely enough people nowadays know what it means to clear away bomb dust and rubble of destruction, making the rough places smooth again. They will know it for many years to come with this labor weighing on them. Oh may the arresting voices of the wilderness ring out warning humankind in good time that ruin and devastation actually spread from within. May the Advent figure of St. John the Baptist, the incorruptible herald and teacher in God's name, be no longer a stranger in our own wilderness. Much depends on such symbolic figures in our lives. For how shall we hear if there are none to cry out, none whose voice can rise above the tumult of violence and destruction, the false clamor that deafens us to reality?[2]

After the Verdict. It has become an odd sort of life I am leading. It is so easy to get used to existence again that one has to keep reminding oneself that death is round the corner. Condemned to death. The thought refuses to penetrate; it almost needs force to drive it home. The thing that makes this kind of death so singular is that one feels so vibrantly alive with the will to live unbroken and every nerve tingling with life. A malevolent external force is the only thing that can end it. The usual intimations of approaching death are therefore lacking. One of these days the door will open, the jailer will say, "Pack up. The car will be here in half an hour." We have often heard this and know exactly what it is like. . . .

Up to now the Lord has helped me wonderfully. I am not yet scared and not yet beaten. The hour of human weakness will no doubt come and sometimes I am depressed when I think of all the things I hoped to do. But I am now a man internally free and far more genuine and realized than I was before. Only now have I sufficient insight to see the thing as a whole.

To be quite honest I do not yet believe in my execution. I don't know why. Perhaps our Father, God, has some great grace in store for me and will enable me to pass through this wilderness without having to perish in it. During the proceedings, even when it was clear there would be no miracle, I felt lifted above it all and quite untouched by all that was going on. Was that a miracle? If not, what was it? I am really in some embarrassment before God and must think it out.

All these long months of misfortune fit into some special pattern. From the first I was so sure everything would turn out well. God always strengthened me in that conviction. These last few days I have doubted and wondered whether my will to live has been sublimated into religious delusions or something like that. Yet all these unmistakable moments of exaltation in the midst of misery; my confidence and unshakable faith even when I was being beaten up, the certain "in spite of it all" that kept my spirits up and made me so sure that they would not succeed in destroying me; those consolations in prayer and in the Blessed Sacrament, the moments of grace; the signs I prayed for that were vouchsafed again and again—must I put them all away from me now? Does God ask the sacrifice which I will not deny him—or is he testing my faith and my trust to the last limit of endurance? . . .

What is God's purpose in all this? Is it a further lesson with regard to complete freedom and absolute surrender? Does he want us to drain the chalice to the dregs and are these hours of waiting preparation for an extraordinary Advent? Or is he testing our faith?

What should I do to remain loyal—go on hoping despite the hopelessness of it all? Or should I relax? Ought I to resign myself to the inevitable and is it cowardice not to do this and to go on hoping? Should I simply stand still, free and ready to take whatever God sends? I can't yet see the way clear before me; I must go on praying for light and guidance. And then there is the accepted sacrifice of the past seven months. It is terrible the way a person keeps on going over these things in his heart. But at least I will look at them honestly under the impulse of the Holy Spirit. . . .

But one thing is gradually becoming clear—I must surrender myself completely. This is seed-time, not harvest. God sows the seed and some time or other he will do the reaping. The one thing I must do is to make sure the seed falls on fertile ground. And I must arm myself against the pain and depression that sometimes almost defeat me. If this is the way God has chosen—and everything indicates that it is—then I must willingly and without rancor make it my way. May others at some future time find it possible to have a better and happier life because we died in this hour of trial.

I ask my friends not to mourn, but to pray for me and help me as long as I have need of help. And to be quite clear in their own minds that I was sacrificed, not conquered. It never occurred to me that my life would end like this. I had spread my sails to the wind and set my course for a great voyage, flags flying, ready to brave every storm that blew. But it could be they were false flags or my course wrongly set or the ship a pirate and its cargo contraband. I don't know. And I will not sink to cheap jibes at the world in order to raise my spirits. To be quite honest I don't want to die, particularly now that I feel I could do more important work and deliver a new message about values I have only just discovered and understood. But it has turned out otherwise. God keep me in his providence and give me strength to meet what is before me.

It only remains for me to thank a great many people for their help and loyalty and belief in me, and for the love they have shown me. First and foremost my brethren in the Order who gave me a genuine and beautiful vision of life. And the many sincere people I was privileged to meet. I remember very clearly the times when we were able to meet freely and discuss the tasks in front of us. Do not give up, ever. Never cease to cherish the people in your hearts—the poor forsaken and betrayed people who are so helpless. For in spite of all their outward display and loud self-assurance, deep down they are lonely and frightened. If through one person's life there is a little more love and kindness, a little more light and truth in the world, then he will not have lived in vain.

Nor must I forget those to whom I owe so much. May those I have hurt forgive me—I am sorry for having injured them. May those to whom I have been untrue forgive me—I am sorry for having failed them. May those to whom I have been proud and overbearing forgive me—I repent my arrogance. And may those to whom I have been unloving forgive me—I repent my hardness. Oh yes—long hours spent in this cell with fettered wrists and my body and spirit tormented must have broken down a great deal that was hard in me. Much that was unworthy and worthless has been committed to the flames.

So farewell. My offense is that I believed in Germany and her eventual emergence from this dark hour of error and distress, that I refused to accept that accumulation of arrogance, pride and force that is the Nazi way of life, and that I did this as a Christian and a Jesuit. These are the values for which I am here now on the brink waiting for the thrust that will send me over. Germany will be reborn, once this time has passed, in a new form based on reality with Christ and his Church recognized again as being the answer to the secret yearning of this earth and its people, with the Order the home of proved men—men who today are hated because they are misunderstood in their voluntary dedication or feared as a reproach in the prevailing state of pathetic, immeasurable human bondage. These are the thoughts with which I go to my death.[3]

Letter to the Brethren

Dear Brethren,

Here I am at the parting of the ways and I must take the other road after all. The death sentence has been passed and the atmosphere is so charged with enmity and hatred that no appeal has any hope of succeeding.

I thank the Order and my brethren for all their goodness and loyalty and help, especially during these last weeks. I ask pardon for much that was untrue and unjust; and I beg that a little help and care may be given to my aged, sick parents.

The actual reason for my condemnation was that I happened to be, and chose to remain, a Jesuit. There was nothing to show that I had any connection with the attempt on Hitler's life so I was acquitted on that count. The rest of the accusations were far less serious and more factual. There was one underlying theme—a Jesuit is *a priori* an enemy and betrayer of the Reich. So the whole proceedings turned into a sort of comedy developing a theme. It was not justice—it was simply the carrying out of the determination to destroy.

May God shield you all. I ask for your prayers. And I will do my best to catch up, on the other side, with all that I have left undone here on earth.

Towards noon I will celebrate Mass once more and then in God's name take the road under his providence and guidance.

In God's blessing and protection,
Your grateful,
Alfred Delp, s.j.[4]

Ignacio Ellacuría (1930–1989)

Ignacio Ellacuría entered the Society of Jesus in Spain during the period following World War II. As a second-year novice he joined the Central American mission in El Salvador. After several years spent studying literature and philosophy in Ecuador and three years teaching at the diocesan seminary in San Salvador, he returned to Europe to study theology under Karl Rahner and complete a doctorate in philosophy under Xavier Zubiri, a renowned Spanish philosopher. He returned to El Salvador in 1967. That tiny country, like much of Latin America, was marked by political repression, inequitable land distribution, chronic unemployment, inadequate housing, illiteracy, poor sanitation and health care, and high rates of infant mortality. The intolerable social reality gave rise to revolutionary ferment that in turn led to increasingly brutal political repression. In 1980 the country exploded, touching off a devastating, twelve-year civil war.

A brilliant thinker, writer, and teacher, Ellacuría became the president of the University of Central America (UCA) just months before the archbishop of San Salvador, Monseñor Oscar Romero, was assassinated while celebrating Mass in 1980. The war began several months later. Ellacuría joined other church leaders in pressing for peace negotiations and an end to government-sponsored repression and violence. As the president of the UCA, he engaged the polarized and deadly political situation of his country with a unique blend of moral authority and theological vision. He empathized with the majority of Salvadorans for whom the war caused terrible suffering and saw clearly the depth of the stalemate between the warring parties. In 1989, with a peace agreement seemingly within reach, yet another round of talks between government and revolutionary leaders broke down. A long-threatened guerrilla offensive was launched. It did not lead to a military victory for either side, but it did give right-wing elements in the military high command a pretext for ordering the grisly midnight assassination of Ellacuría, five other Jesuit priests, a seminary cook, and her daughter.

Ellacuría's academic career unfolded in the dramatic context of his life. Despite the pressures he faced he found time to produce several books and over two hundred articles on a range of topics, exploring in depth the political implications of Christian faith and the philosophical foundations of Christian theology. We have organized selections from his writings into two thematic sections. "Meditations at the Foot of the Cross" includes six selections focusing on the central Christian symbol of the cross, beginning with an adaptation of a colloquy from the *Spiritual Exercises* where Ignatius instructs the believer to kneel before the crucified and ask, "What have I done for Christ? What am I doing for Christ? What ought I to do for Christ?" (SpEx 53). The second selection points to the historical reasons for Jesus' death. The third and fourth selections touch on the original (and dangerous) phrase developed by Ellacuría, "the crucified people." The final two selections develop Ellacuría's theological conviction that the poor in our world afford the best place—"the foot of the cross"—to encounter God.

The second section, "Salvation in History," focuses on the relationship between Christian salvation and historical liberation, a theme Ellacuría calls "historical soteriology." The first three excerpts link God's salvation revealed in Jesus to the ongoing historical liberation that incarnates that salvation today. The final selection recapitulates this understanding of salvation in a passage that serves as Ellacuría's own "definition" of liberation theology.

Kevin F. Burke, s.j.

Meditations at the Foot of the Cross (From *Escritos Teológicos* and *Mysterium Liberationis*)

What I would ask—because the word "demand" sounds too strong—involves two things. First, that you look with your eyes and heart at these peoples who are suffering so much—some from poverty and hunger, others from oppression and repression. Then, because I am a Jesuit, I would bid you pray the colloquy of St. Ignatius from the first week of the Exercises before this crucified people, asking yourself: What have I done to crucify them? What am I doing to end their crucifixion? What should I do so that this people might rise from the dead?[1]

***

The "why did Jesus die" cannot be explained apart from the "why did they kill him." Moreover, the historical priority must be sought in the "why did they kill him." They killed Jesus for the life that he lived and for the mission that he carried out. This "why" of his death can be posed in terms of the "for what reason" of his death. If, from a theological-historical point of view it can be said that Jesus died for our sins and for human salvation, from a historical-theological point of view it must be maintained that they killed him for the life he lived.[2]

***

Among so many signs always being given, some identified and others hardly perceptible, there is in every age one that is primary, in whose light we should discern and interpret all the rest. This perennial sign is the historically crucified people, who link their permanence to ever distinct forms of their crucifixion. This crucified people represents the historical continuation of the servant of Yahweh, who is forever being stripped of his human features by the sin of the world, who is forever being despoiled of everything by the powerful of this world, who is forever being robbed even of life, especially of life.[3]

***

We should acknowledge a trans-historic dimension in Jesus' activity, as we should acknowledge it in his personal biography, but this trans-historic dimension will only be real if it is indeed trans-historic, that is, if it goes through history. Hence, we must ask who continues to carry out in history what his life and death was about.

We can approach the question by taking into account that there is a crucified people, whose crucifixion is the product of actions in history. . . .

What is meant by crucified people here is that collective body, which as the majority of humankind owes its situation of crucifixion to the way society is organized and maintained by a minority that exercises its dominion through a series of factors, which taken together and given their concrete impact within history, must be regarded as sin.[4]

***

It is said that in cultures that have grown old there is no longer a place for [the prophetic way of life] and utopia, but only for pragmatism and selfishness, for the countable verification of results, for the scientific calculation of input and output, or, at best, for institutionalizing, legalizing, and ritualizing the spirit that renews all things. Whether this situation is inevitable or not, there are nonetheless still places where hope is not simply the cynical adding up of infinitesimal calculations; they are places to hope and to give hope against all the dogmatic verdicts that shut the door on the future of utopia and [the prophetic way of life] and the struggle.

One of these places is Latin America.[5]

***

The poor of Latin America are a theological place insofar as they constitute the maximum and scandalous, prophetic, and apocalyptic presence of the Christian God and, consequently, the privileged place of Christian praxis and reflection. . . . Here, *theological place* is understood . . . to be the place where the God of Jesus was made manifest in a special way because this was as the Father wanted it. He is manifested not only by way of relevant clarification, but also by way of a call to conversion. The two aspects are strictly intertwined. Without conversion to the poor as the place where God reveals himself and calls us, one does not adequately approach the living reality of God and his clarifying light. Without the presence and grace of God that is given to us in and through the poor, conversion is not fully possible.

Now, this special presence of God—of the God of Jesus in the historical reality of the poor—has its own configuration, through which it is distinguished from other real presences of Jesus, the Son of God . . . as the place where the Christian God makes himself most luminous and living. It is initially a hidden and disconcerting presence that has very similar characteristics to that which was the hidden and disconcerting presence of the Son of God in the historical flesh of Jesus of Nazareth. A prophetic presence immediately follows which utters its first word in the naked manifestation of its own reality, and its second word in the announcement of its own properly Christian reality that seeks to wipe out the sin of the world. It is, finally, an apocalyptic presence because in many ways it helps consummate the end of this time of oppression, while with labor pains and chilling signs it points to the birth of a new humanity, a new earth, and a new age. A hidden, scandalous presence, a prophetic presence, and an apocalyptic presence are three essential characteristics of this theological place that is particular to the poor.[6]

Salvation in History (From *Freedom Made Flesh* and *Mysterium Liberationis*)

But it is not just that there is a salvation history. There is also the fact that salvation must be historical. This implies two things: 1) Salvation will differ with the time and place in which it is fleshed out; 2) it must be fleshed out in history, in human beings who live in history. Salvation cannot be defined in univocal terms. Nor can it be defined as if [the human being] were a spirit without history, a spirit who is not incarnated in history. Nor can it be defined as if salvation in the "hereafter" were not supposed to be signified and signalized in the "here and now."[7]

***

An historical understanding of salvation cannot theorize abstractly on the essence of salvation. Not only is that abstract theorizing more historical than it appears, and as abstraction it can deny the real meaning of salvation, but it is also impossible to speak of salvation except in terms of concrete situations. Salvation is always the salvation *of someone*, and *of something* in that person. This is so much so that the characteristics of the savior must be understood in terms of the characteristics of that which needs saving. This would seem to diminish the meaning of salvation as the gift of God, who anticipates the needs of humanity, but it does not. It does not, because the needs, understood in their broadest sense, are the historical path by which we move toward the recognition of that gift, which will appear as a "negation" of the needs, because from the perspective of that gift the needs appear as a "negation" of the gift of God, of God's self-giving to humanity. But beyond that, the needs can be seen as the outcry of God made flesh in human suffering, as the unmistakable voice of God, who moans in pain in God's own creatures, or more exactly, in God's children.[8]

***

Granting that there may be a difference between salvation history and real history as it is lived empirically, we can say that at bottom believers see these two histories as one, that is, united in what might be called the great history of God. This perception presupposes that history is presented as a whole, with two parts. The first is what can be called salvation history, which certainly is not limited to sacramental or cultic or strictly religious life. The second, which has a more profane appearance, is also part of the great history of God with humanity. . . .

Therefore the Kingdom of Heaven is, in a first moment, a seed sown in the fields of the world and in history, to make it a history of God, of a God who is definitively all in all. In this first moment the field is not subjected to the seed, but the seed to the field; or, as the other evangelical parable puts it, the leavening of the Kingdom is modestly and effectively mixed into the dough of the world to make it ferment and rise.

All this is expressed with absolute naturalness in the relationship of the believing people of Latin America to nature and to one another. To be committed only to the religious aspect of the Kingdom, without concern for its essential reference to the world and history, would be a clear betrayal of God's history; it would leave the field of history to God's enemies. This is not reductionism, either reducing God's history to the history of Christian salvation in its restricted sense or reducing God's history to the history of political, social, economic, or cultural events. Rather, it is an attempt through Christian faith and action in the midst of the world—which has its own autonomy just as Christian faith and action have—to build God's history, in which Christ's action and human actions, the dictates of faith and of reason, come together in their different forms and different levels of reality.[9]

***

The theology of liberation understands itself as a reflection from faith on the historical reality and action of the people of God, who follow the work of Jesus in announcing and fulfilling [God's Reign]. It understands itself as an action by the people of God in following the work of Jesus and, as Jesus did, it tries to establish a living connection between the world of God and the human world. Its reflective character does not keep it from being an action, and an action by the people of God, even though at times it is forced to make use of theoretical tools that seem to remove it both from immediate action and from the theoretical discourse that is popular elsewhere. It is, thus, a theology that begins with historical acts and seeks to lead to historical acts, and therefore it is not satisfied with being a purely interpretive reflection; it is nourished by faithful belief in the presence of God within history, an operative presence that, although it must be grasped in grateful faith, remains a historical action. There is no room here for faith without works; rather, that faith draws the believers into the very force of God that operates in history, so that we are converted into new historical forms of that operative and salvific presence of God in humanity.[10]

PART V
SCHOLARSHIP

Although Jesuits are linked in the minds of many with schools, education, and scholarship, the Society of Jesus was not founded to be a teaching order. The early Society initially opened small schools only to educate young men who came to join the community. But by 1547, seven years after the founding of the Society, a papal order was given to the general to depute members of the Society to teach theology and all other disciplines. By 1560, four years after Ignatius' death, the ministry of education was accounted equal in importance to all the other ministries together. Thus, in just two decades after its founding, the Society had become a major force in education and scholarly research throughout Europe and in the mission lands.

The list of important Jesuit scholars through the years includes mathematicians, scientists, linguists, cartographers, political theorists, philosophers, and theologians. Figures like Peter Canisius, Christopher Clavius, Robert Bellarmine, Francisco Suárez, Athanasius Kircher, Roger Boscovich, Angelo Secchi, John LaFarge, and John Courtney Murray stand out but do not stand alone in their scholarly brilliance and social contributions. Included on this list are Pierre Teilhard de Chardin, Bernard Lonergan, and Karl Rahner, three Jesuits whose ability to link theology with other fields of modern scholarship helped the church to build valuable bridges between its biblical and practical tradition and the contemporary world. Steeped in the Ignatian imperative to "find God in all things," their writings integrate faith with reason, philosophy with science, and theology with anthropology. In this they help Christians encounter the scientific, postmodern world with radical intellectual honesty.

Eileen Burke-Sullivan and Kevin F. Burke, s.j.

Pierre Teilhard de Chardin (1881–1955)

Like a man born out of time, Pierre Teilhard de Chardin grew up in the late nineteenth century—the years immediately following the First Vatican Council (1869–1870). He lived through the dramatic years of the first half of the twentieth century and died in the decade before the dawn of Vatican II (1962–1965). A brilliant scientist, philosopher, and theologian, he felt compelled to push for the reconciliation of faith and science—one of the hallmarks of the Catholic Church *after* Vatican II— during the chilly period of rigid apologetics that dominated the church *before* that great council. As a result, he was forever misunderstood within his own church and virtually exiled within his own religious family. With hindsight we can now see the depth with which he grasped and lived the Ignatian charism. For all of the limitations of his particular attempt to engender a reconciliation of evolutionary theory and Christian dogma, we can also discern the truth in his basic intuitions, the intuitions of a genuine Ignatian mystic. Finally, we encounter in him the capacity to overcome everything through the *practice* of hope-filled faith, discrete charity, discernment, and forgiveness.

Teilhard de Chardin lived a life at once dramatic and quietly ordinary. He entered the Jesuits in 1899 and after his ordination served as a stretcher bearer in the First World War. (During this time he composed a series of haunting essays later published as *Writings in Time of War*.) Along with the usual Jesuit training in the humanities, philosophy, and theology, Teilhard also pursued specialized studies in science and eventually concentrated in geology and paleontology. In 1923 he made his first trip to China but on his return to France was barred from teaching because of suspicion aroused by his way of integrating faith and science around such tricky issues as the meaning of original sin. He returned to China in 1926 and spent the bulk of the next twenty years there. After suffering a heart attack in 1947 he returned to France in 1948 and sought permission to publish his major recent work (*The Phenomenon of Man*) and to resume his teaching career there. Both requests were denied and Teilhard lived in the United States (traveling to South Africa, South America, and Europe) until his death in New York City on Easter Sunday, 1955.

The life of Pierre Teilhard de Chardin testifies in a profound and distinctive way to the centrality of the Ignatian imperative "to find God in all things." Likewise, this theme runs through all of his scientific, philosophical, theological, and mystical writings. This theme appears with striking new valences in the three selections gathered under the Ignatian theme, "Finding God in All Things." Taken from his evocative work, *The Divine Milieu* (1956), all three selections were written in China and France in the late 1920s, but, like nearly all of Teilhard's writings, they were published only after his death in 1955.

Throughout his life Teilhard de Chardin hoped to harmonize revealed truth with the world disclosed by science. His own life story witnesses to the cost he paid for this hope. He was regarded with suspicion by church authorities and dismissed by scientific authorities. Ironically, even as the theological vision of the Second Vatican Council has created a new openness toward his theological intuitions, recent advances in biology and physics are beginning to verify many of his groundbreaking scientific intuitions. The excerpts contained in "Science and Faith" give evidence of Teilhard's passion to bring these two interests together, a passion fed by deep Ignatian roots. Today, more than fifty years after his death, his insights speak gently and powerfully to a world still troubled by the false dichotomy underlying the alleged opposition between science and religion.

The final section focuses on Teilhard's "Patient Trust in God." The first of these two beautiful reflections is a prayer for trust in the face of the terrifying reality of having been born; it gives eloquent witness to the God he believed in. The second is taken from a letter to his beloved cousin, Marguerite Teilhard-Chambon. In it, Teilhard extols the virtue of patience, the same generous patience with which he was blessed to live.

Kevin F. Burke, S.J.

Finding God in All Things (From *The Divine Milieu*)

All around us, to right and left, in front and behind, above and below, we have only had to go a little beyond the frontier of sensible appearances in order to see the divine welling up and showing through. But it is not only close to us, in front of us, that the divine Presence has revealed itself. It has sprung up universally, and we find ourselves so surrounded and transfixed by it, that there is no room left to fall down and adore it, even within ourselves.

By means of all created things, without exception, the divine assails us, penetrates us and moulds us. We imagined it as distant and inaccessible, whereas in fact we live steeped in its burning layers. *In eo vivimus* [In him we live]. As Jacob said, awakening from his dream, the world, this palpable world, to which we brought the boredom and callousness reserved for profane places, is in truth a holy place, and we did not know it. *Venite, adoremus* [Come, let us adore].[1]

***

The essential marvel of the divine milieu is the ease with which it assembles and harmonises within itself qualities which appear to us to be contradictory.

As vast as the world and much more formidable than the most immense energies of the universe, it nevertheless possesses in a supreme degree the concentration and the specific qualities which are the charm and warmth of human persons.

Vast and innumerable as the dazzling surge of creatures that are sustained and sur-animated by its ocean, it nevertheless retains the concrete transcendence that allows it to bring back the elements of the world, without the least confusion, within its triumphant and personal unity.

Incomparably near and perceptible—for it presses in upon us through all the forces of the universe—it nevertheless eludes our grasp so constantly that we can never seize it here below except by raising ourselves, uplifted on its waves, to the extreme limit of our efforts: present in, and drawing at the inaccessible depth of, each creature, it withdraws always further, bearing us along with it towards the common centre of all consummation.[2]

***

To have access to the divine milieu is to have found the One Thing needful: *Him who burns* by setting fire to everything that we would love badly or not enough; *Him who calms* by eclipsing with His blaze everything that we would love too much; *Him who consoles* by gathering up everything that has been snatched from our love or has never been given to it. To reach those priceless layers is to experience, with equal truth, that one has need of everything, and that one has need of nothing. Everything is needed because the world will never be large enough to provide our taste for action with the means of grasping God, or our thirst for undergoing with the possibility of being invaded by Him. And yet nothing is needed; for as the only reality which can satisfy us lies beyond the transparencies in which it is mirrored, everything that fades away and dies between us will only serve to give reality back to us with greater purity. Everything means both everything and nothing to me; everything is God to me and everything is dust to me: that is what [a person] can say with equal truth, in accord with how the divine ray falls.[3]

Science and Faith (From *The Phenomenon of Man, The Divine Milieu,* and *Toward the Future*)

How can we account for that irresistible instinct in our hearts which leads us towards unity whenever and in whatever direction our passions are stirred? A sense of the universe, a sense of the *all*, the nostalgia which seizes us when confronted by nature, beauty, music—these seem to be an expectation and awareness of a Great Presence. The "mystics" and their commentators apart, how has psychology been able so consistently to ignore this fundamental vibration whose ring can be heard by every practised ear at the basis, or rather at the summit, of every great emotion? Resonance to the All—the keynote of pure poetry and pure religion. Once again: what does this phenomenon, which is born with thought and grows with it, reveal if not a deep accord between two realities which seek each other; the severed particle which trembles at the approach of "the rest"?[4]

***

To outward appearance, the modern world was born of an antireligious movement: [the human person] becoming self-sufficient and reason supplanting belief. Our generation and the two that preceded it have heard little but talk of the conflict between science and faith; indeed it seemed at one moment a foregone conclusion that the former was destined to take the place of the latter.

But, inasmuch as the tension is prolonged, the conflict visibly seems to need to be resolved in terms of an entirely different form of equilibrium—not in elimination, nor duality, but in synthesis. After close on two centuries of passionate struggles, neither science nor faith has succeeded in discrediting its adversary. On the contrary, it becomes obvious that neither can develop normally without the other. And the reason is simple: the same life animates both. Neither in its impetus nor its achievements can science go to its limits without becoming tinged with mysticism and charged with faith.[5]

***

Faith, as we understand it here, is not—of course—simply the intellectual adherence to Christian dogma. It is taken in a much richer sense to mean belief in God charged with all the trust in [God's] beneficent strength that the knowledge of the divine Being arouses in us. It means the practical conviction that the universe, between the hands of the Creator, still continues to be the clay in which [the Creator] shapes innumerable possibilities according to His will.[6]

***

What paralyzes life is lack of faith and lack of audacity. The difficulty lies not in solving problems but in identifying them. And so we cannot avoid this conclusion: it is biologically evident that to gain control of passion and so make it serve spirit must be a condition of progress. Sooner or later, then, the world will brush aside our incredulity and take this step, because whatever is truer comes out into the open and whatever is better is ultimately realized.

The day will come when, after harnessing space, the winds, the tides, gravitation, we shall harness for God the energies of love. And, on that day, for the second time in the history of the world, human beings will have discovered fire.[7]

Patient Trust in God (From *Hymn of the Universe* and *The Making of a Mind*)

It is a terrifying thing to have been born I mean, to find oneself, without having willed it, swept irrevocably along on a torrent of fearful energy which seems as though it wished to destroy everything it carries with it.

What I want, my God, is that by a reversal of forces which you alone can bring about, my terror in the face of the nameless changes destined to renew my being may be turned into an overflowing joy at being transformed into you.[8]

***

Above all, trust in the *slow* work of God. We are, quite naturally, impatient in everything to reach the end without delay. We should like to skip the intermediate stages. We are impatient of being *on the way to* something *unknown*, something *new*. And yet it is the law of all progress that it is made by passing through some stage of instability—and that it may take a very long time. . . .

And so, I think, it is with you. Your ideas mature gradually—let them grow, let them shape themselves, without undue haste. Don't try to "force" them on, as though you could be today what time (that is to say, grace and circumstances acting on your own good will) will make of you tomorrow. Only God could say what this new spirit gradually forming within you will be. Give our Lord the benefit of believing that his hand is leading you, and accept the anxiety of feeling yourself in suspense and incomplete.[9]

Bernard Lonergan (1904–1984)

Bernard Lonergan was born, raised, and initially educated in Canada. He entered the Jesuits at the age of eighteen and was ordained in 1936. From his youth he was interested in mathematics and science, as well as history and sociology. These latter topics led him to Kant, Hegel, Marx, and Newman, enabling him to wrestle with the inadequacy of classical culture and neoscholastic metaphysics in the intellectual world he inhabited. As his interests in philosophy and theology were more fully aroused in the Society, he became passionately interested in developing a philosophy of history. At the same time, in his early doctoral studies he sought to understand the ways human beings know and understand anything.

During the forties, while teaching at Jesuit seminaries in Canada, Lonergan immersed himself in the thought of Thomas Aquinas, particularly Aquinas' anthropology and epistemology. But it was an Aquinas entered from a thoroughly modern sociological and historical perspective rather than what Lonergan calls a classicist framework. Armed with a new understanding of history he traced how dramatically historical consciousness was changing the face of theological writing.

As a theological advisor for the Canadian bishops at Vatican II, Lonergan met virtually every important theologian of the era. In the context of seemingly endless and often fruitless debates about theology he discovered the importance of an adequate cognitional theory and theological method for ongoing theological development. In his last two decades he focused on the way meaning—which is shaped by historical circumstances—is constitutive of human institutions. In light of this awareness Lonergan noted that his whole lifework was introducing history into Catholic theology. He continued to study, to lecture, and to teach these central themes nearly to the end of his life.

We provide two brief excerpts from Lonergan's impressive corpus. The first appears under the theme of "Human Development" and comes from Lonergan's most important work, *Insight: A Study of Human Understanding* (1957). In this brilliant and sustained work of philosophy, Lonergan spends ten chapters developing a series of intellectual exercises that "assist the reader in effecting a personal appropriation of the concrete, dynamic structure immanent and recurrently operative in his own cognitional activities." In chapters 11–20 he capitalizes on this cognitional analysis to address the fundamental questions of metaphysics, ethics, and philosophy of God. The current selection comes from chapter 15, "Elements of Metaphysics," where he utilizes a genetic method to account for development in general and human development in particular.

The second section, "Theology in Its New Context," addresses Lonergan's desire to develop an account of theological method capable of addressing the challenges of modern epistemology. In the years following the publication of *Insight* and especially in the wake of the Second Vatican Council (1962–1965) he focused primarily on this task. This stage in his career culminated with the publication of his second masterpiece, *Method in Theology* (1974). In this book he argues that "a theology mediates between a cultural matrix and the significance and role of a religion in that matrix."[1] The selection presented here does not come from *Method in Theology* but from a paper Lonergan gave to a conference on religious renewal in 1968 while he was writing that book. In this selection he addresses the need for theology to move from classical to empirical conceptions of culture.

Eileen Burke-Sullivan and Kevin F. Burke, s.j.

From "Human Development" in *Insight*

Organic, psychic, and intellectual development are not three independent processes. They are interlocked with the intellectual providing a higher integration of the psychic and the psychic providing a higher integration of the organic. Each level involves its own laws, its flexible circle of schemes of recurrence, its interlocked set of conjugate forms. Each set of forms stands in an emergent correspondence to otherwise coincidental manifolds on the lower levels. Hence, a single human action can involve a series of components, physical, chemical, organic, neural, psychic, and intellectual; and the several components occur in accord with the laws and realized schemes of their appropriate levels. However, while physical and chemical laws are static, higher correlations pertain to systems on the move, and quite obviously, there results the problem of formulating the heuristic structure of the investigation of this triply compounded development. What the existentialist discovers and talks about, what the ascetic attempts to achieve in himself, what the psychiatrist endeavours to foster in another, what the psychologist aims at understanding completely, the metaphysician outlines in heuristic categories.

First, then, at any stage of his development a man is an individual, existing unity differentiated by physical, chemical, organic, psychic, and intellectual conjugates. . . .

Secondly, man develops. Whatever he is at present, he was not always so, and generally speaking he need not remain so. . . .

Thirdly, there is a law of integration. The initiative of development may be organic, psychic, intellectual, or external, but the development remains fragmentary until the principle of correspondence between different levels is satisfied. . . .

Fourthly, there is a law of limitation and transcendence. It is a law of tension. On the one hand, development is in the subject and of the subject; on the other hand, it is from the subject as he is and towards the subject as he is to be. . . .

Fifthly, there is a law of genuineness. At first sight it is an obvious matter of simplicity and honesty, of perspicacity and sincerity. But a little probing brings to light a paradox. In so far as development occurs non-consciously, there is no relevance to genuineness, for simplicity and honesty, perspicacity and sincerity, are qualities of conscious acts. On the other hand, one may argue, the more consciously a development occurs, the less the likelihood that it will be marked by genuineness, for when one speaks of a simple and honest soul, one is not thinking of a person given to deep and prolonged self-scrutiny. . . .

So there emerges into consciousness a concrete apprehension of an obviously practicable and proximate ideal self; but along with it there also emerges the tension between limitation and transcendence; and it is no vague tension between limitation in general and transcendence in general, but an unwelcome invasion of consciousness by opposed apprehensions of oneself as one concretely is and as one concretely is to be.

Genuineness is the admission of that tension into consciousness, and so it is the necessary condition of the harmonious co-operation of the conscious and unconscious components of development. It does not brush questions aside, smother doubts, push problems down, escape to activity, to chatter, to passive entertainment, to sleep, to narcotics. It confronts issues, inspects them, studies their many aspects, works out their various implications, contemplates their concrete consequences in one's own life and in the lives of others. If it respects inertial tendencies as necessary conservative forces, it does not conclude that a defective routine is to be maintained because one has grown accustomed to it. Though it fears the cold plunge into becoming other than one is, it does not dodge the issue, nor pretend bravery, nor act out of bravado. It is capable of assurance and confidence, not only in what has been tried and found successful, but also in what is yet to be tried. It grows weary with the perpetual renewal of further questions to be faced, it longs for rest, it falters and it fails, but it knows its weakness and its failures and it does not try to rationalize them.[2]

From "Theology in Its New Context" in *A Second Collection*

Any theology of renewal goes hand in hand with a renewal of theology. For "renewal" is being used in a novel sense. Usually in Catholic circles "renewal" has meant a return to the olden times of pristine virtue and deep wisdom. But good Pope John has made "renewal" mean *"aggiornamento,"* "bringing things up to date."

Obviously, if theology is to be brought up to date, it must have fallen behind the times. Again, if we are to know what is to be done to bring theology up to date, we must ascertain when it began to fall behind the times, in what respects it got out of touch, in what respects it failed to meet the issues and effect the developments that long ago were due and now are long overdue.

The answer I wish to suggest takes us back almost three centuries to the end of the seventeenth century. . . .

It would be unfair to expect the theologians of the end of the seventeenth century to have discerned the good and the evil in the great movements of their time. But at least we may record what in fact they did do. They introduced "dogmatic" theology. It is true that the word "dogmatic" had been previously applied to theology. But then it was used to denote a distinction from moral, or ethical, or historical theology. Now it was employed in new sense, in opposition to scholastic theology. It replaced the inquiry of the *quaestio* by the pedagogy of the thesis. It demoted the quest of faith for understanding to a desirable, but secondary, and indeed, optional goal. It gave basic and central significance to the certitudes of faith, their presuppositions, and their consequences. It owed its mode of proof to Melchior Cano and, as that theologian was also a bishop and inquisitor, so the new dogmatic theology not only proved its theses, but also was supported by the teaching authority and the sanctions of the Church.

Such a conception of theology survived right into the twentieth century, and even today in some circles it is the only conception that is understood. Still, among theologians its limitations and defects have been becoming more and more apparent, especially since the 1890's. During the last seventy years, efforts to find remedies and to implement them have been going forward steadily, if unobtrusively. The measure of their success is the radically new situation brought to light by the Second Vatican Council.

There is, perhaps, no need for me here to insist that the novelty resides not in a new revelation or a new faith, but in a new cultural context. For a theology is a product not only of the religion it investigates and expounds but also of the cultural ideals and norms that set its problems and direct its solutions. Just as theology in the thirteenth century followed its age by assimilating Aristotle, just as theology in the seventeenth century resisted its age by retiring into a dogmatic corner, so theology today is locked in an encounter with its age. Whether it will grow and triumph, or whether it will wither to insignificance, depends in no small measure on the clarity and the accuracy of its grasp of the external cultural factors that undermine its past achievements and challenge it to new endeavors.[3]

Karl Rahner (1904–1984)

Karl Rahner was born in Freiburg im Breisgau, Germany, on March 5, 1904, the same year that Bernard Lonergan, John Courtney Murray, and Yves Congar were born. At the age of eighteen he followed his older brother Hugo into the Society of Jesus and after his ordination in 1932 he matriculated at the University of Freiburg to secure a doctorate in philosophy. Just before completing his dissertation he was notified of its rejection by his committee. In just nine months, Rahner wrote another doctoral dissertation in theology on a passage from John's gospel. His rejected philosophical dissertation was published two years later and translated into several languages. The war interfered with his teaching career when the Nazis expelled the Jesuits from their schools, so Rahner joined the diocesan pastoral institute in Vienna for six years, only returning to university teaching in the late forties after the war.

In his early teaching Rahner was confronted with the terrible state of official theology in the Catholic Church. He asked whether anyone who seriously thinks can live the Christian existence today with intellectual honesty. The theology being taught in seminaries was not coherent with modern life and was therefore incapable of being pastorally meaningful. For Rahner the crux of the issue lay in finding a reasonable voice for Catholic doctrine that sustained both the unity and comprehensiveness of the faith but described it in terms that are reasonable and credible to ordinary believers of the post-Enlightenment world. He wanted to facilitate the "translation" of Christian revelation into modern concepts, especially with a modern philosophical base.

Rahner took up the question, what are the conditions of the possibility for human beings to grasp the revelation of the mystery of God? He then established that those conditions lie within the believer first of all. A possibility for self-transcendence is found in every human being who has ever imagined something beyond his or her own immediate capability or possession. One need not be a brilliant philosopher or saintly mystic to know the pull toward self-transcendence, but one must be attentive to it, and to the truth that lies just beyond the possibilities that we actually reach.

Rahner became one of the most influential theological voices in the whole Christian Church of the second half of the twentieth century, and he served as the most famous theological advisor for the bishops at the Second Vatican Council. The sheer volume of his nearly four thousand published works, coupled with the breadth of the topics he addressed, partially accounts for his enormous authority in Catholic theological circles, and his extended influence among other Christians as well. As with Teilhard and Lonergan, it is impossible to do justice to Rahner's enormous intellectual achievement through a few pages excerpted from his writings. As the brief selection below indicates, however, the Ignatian vision is central to all of his thought.

Toward the end of his life Karl Rahner was asked to write an extended preface for a pictorial biography [*farbige Bildband*] of St. Ignatius.[1] The selection presented below, "Ignatius Speaks to a Jesuit Today," is taken from this work. Because he wanted to address the question of the relevance of Ignatius for our day, Rahner chose to write an imaginary piece where Ignatius speaks in the first person to a contemporary Jesuit. He did so, however, with this important disclaimer: "What I say in this regard or have Ignatius say, is of course not an official position or plan on the part of the Order, but rather only my own private, subjective opinion, and I present it fully aware that it is given in a subjective, selective way and that I cannot say everything that ought to be said or even that I would like to say." In this selection we see Rahner touching on three crucial Ignatian themes: the possibility of having an immediate experience of God, the ecclesial implications of this possible encounter, and the centrality of Jesus as the concrete "event" of God's absolute inclining toward the world.

Eileen Burke-Sullivan and Kevin F. Burke, s.j.

From "Ignatius Speaks to a Jesuit Today" in *Schriften zur Theologie XV*

The Immediate Experience of God

You know that I wanted, as I used to say, "to help souls," that is to tell men and women some things about God and God's grace, about

Jesus Christ, the crucified and risen one, things that had the goal of redeeming their freedom into the freedom of God. I wanted to say these things as they had always been said in the Church, and yet I thought (and I was correct in this) that I could say the old anew. Why? I was convinced that I had experienced God immediately, at first as a beginner on my sickbed at Loyola, and then in a decisive way during my stay at Manresa. And I wanted, as far as possible, to communicate this experience to others.

If I claim that I have experienced God immediately, this does not need to be bound up with a theological lecture on the nature of such an immediate experience of God. Neither, then, will I talk about the phenomena that accompanied this experience, which obviously also manifest their particular historical and individual character. I will not talk about my visions, with their images, of the symbols and apparitions, nor of the gift of tears and things of that sort. I will simply say this: I have experienced God, the nameless and unfathomable, holding silent, and yet near, in the triunity of God's self-bestowal to me. I have also and above all experienced God beyond anything the imagination can formulate. God, who, approaching us from out of God's very self in grace, can never be confused with anything else.

Such a conviction might sound quite harmless to you, with all of your pious hustle and bustle, couched in the sublimest words possible. Yet at root it is an outrageous claim, and this both from my perspective [of the beatific vision],[2] where it is possible to experience the inconceivability of God in yet another, and wholly different way, and from the point of view of the godlessness of your own time, in which this godlessness has really only abolished the gods which the previous age—so innocently and yet at the same time so devastatingly—had identified with the unspeakable God. Why shouldn't I say: godlessness even in the Church itself, given that in the final analysis the Church, throughout its history, in unity with the crucified one, is supposed to be the event of the overthrowing of the gods?

Have you never really been shocked that I said in my *Autobiography* that my mysticism had given me such a certainty of the faith that it would remain unshaken even if there were no Holy Scripture? Would it not be easy to charge this with being a subjectivistic mysticism, divorced from the Church? It was not at all such a surprise to me that people in Alcalá, in Salamanca, and elsewhere, suspected me of being an Alumbrado. I have actually met God, the true and living one, the one worthy of the Name that extinguishes all of these names. It makes no difference here whether one wants to call this experience mysticism or something else; how it is possible to clarify to some degree in human concepts how something like this can happen at all—this is something that your theologians can speculate about. . . .

Ignatian Spirituality

It seems to me that . . . this quite simple, and yet entirely outrageous conviction is the kernel of what you are in the habit of calling my spirituality. Seen in and from the perspective of the history of piety within the Church, is this something old or new? Self-evident or shocking? Does it mark the beginning of "modernity" in the Church, and is it perhaps more akin to the fundamental experiences of Luther and Descartes than you Jesuits have wanted to admit down through the centuries? Is it something that will always retreat into the background in the Church, both today and tomorrow, whenever people find themselves almost unable to bear any longer the silent solitude before God, and try to take flight into an ecclesial communitarianism, even though the latter really ought to be made up of spiritual persons who have encountered God immediately, rather than of people who use the Church in order finally not to have to have anything to do with God and God's free inconceivability? My friend, for me such questioning has come to an end, and thus I no longer need the answers. Here I am no prophet of the coming history of the Church. However, you must pose these questions to yourselves and answer them, with theological clarity and, at the same time, in a historical verdict.

But this remains: the human person can experience God God's self. And your pastoral work, in all of its stages and in its goals, ought to keep this fact inexorably in view. If you were to fill up the barns of human consciousness only with your theology, however learned and modernized, in such a way that finally only engenders a horrible torrent of words, if you were only to break people in[3] for the Church and its culture, training them to be enthusiastic underlings in the ecclesial establishment, if you were only to turn men and women in the Church into obedient followers of a far-away God who would be represented by an ecclesial superior, if you were not to help men and women get beyond all of this, if you were not to help them finally let go of every conceptual certainty and particular insight, in a trusting fall into that inconceivability in which there are no longer any paths, if you were not to help bring this about in the deepest, most frightening hopelessness of life, as well as in the measurelessness of love and of joy, and then in a radical and definitive way in death (with the Jesus dying forsaken by God), then really in all of your so-called pastoral work and missionary tasks you would have forgotten or betrayed my "spirituality."

All men and women are sinners and short-sighted, and given this it is my opinion that you Jesuits have not infrequently in your history been guilty of such forgetfulness and betrayal. You have not infrequently defended the Church as if it were the Ultimate, as if the Church were not, in the final analysis, when it is being true to its own essence, the event in which the person gives him or herself over in silence to God, finally without desiring to know at all any more what he or she is doing in this, because God is precisely the inconceivable mystery, and only thus can be our goal and our blessedness. . . .

Jesus

Ever since my conversion Jesus was for me always *the* absolute inclining of God toward the world and toward me, *the* inclining, in which the inconceivability of the pure mystery is wholly there and the man Jesus comes to his own full perfection. The particularity of Jesus never bothered me at all, nor the necessity of seeking him in a specific treasure-trove of events and words, with the intention of finding in these small things the infiniteness of the unspeakable mystery. The journey to Palestine was really able to be for me a journey into the pathlessness of God, and you (not I) are the ones who are simplistic and superficial when you think that my longing for the Holy Land for almost fifteen years is a quirk of a medieval man or something like the longing that a Muslim has today for Mecca. My yearning for the Holy Land was a longing for a Jesus who is concrete, who is no abstract idea.

There is no Christianity that can find the inconceivable God by going around Jesus. God has willed that many, unspeakably many, find God because they are only *seeking* Jesus and, when they collapse in death, are dying with Jesus in his God-forsakenness, even if they are not able to name their destiny using this blessed name. This is because God has only allowed this darkness of finitude and sin into God's world because God makes it God's own in Jesus.

PART VI
IMAGINATION

The Spiritual Exercises of St. Ignatius manifest many fresh and surprising features. Among the most surprising and refreshing: they encourage the follower of Jesus to use his or her imagination in prayer and in the life of faith. Ignatian spirituality does not require people to empty their minds of images. Rather, as William Lynch will say, it encourages them to use the imagination to enter "the valley of the human" so as to find God there. Imagination is not primarily geared to help us escape from reality. On the contrary, it orients us to reality. We use the imagination to construct images (real images) of the world (the real world). As with the Exercises, so too with the entire spirituality that flows from them: early Jesuits in Europe wrote plays, painted masterpieces, and built churches; Jesuit missionaries in Paraguay taught Guaraní Indians how to make violins and play them. They engaged imagination to build a world for faith.

In these chapters devoted to imagination and reality, we look at three Jesuits—a painter, a poet, and a public intellectual. They show us that the production of works of art is a sacred work that takes us deeper into the real, not away from it. They tell us that reflection on beauty, on human complexity, and even on evil, takes us to the very heart of the Christian mystery. Of course, Ignatian spirituality represents but one small expression of the vast Christian tradition of artistic achievement and aesthetic appreciation. But one cannot adequately grasp this distinctive spirituality without pondering its unique contribution to the history of art, drama, sculpture, poetry, music, dance, architecture, and literature—indeed the whole panoply of imaginative artistic expression—and to the way such arts have broadened and deepened our sense of both the human and the world.

Kevin F. Burke, s.j.

Daniel Seghers (1590–1661)

D aniel Seghers was born in Antwerp, Flanders, a century after Igna-tius of Loyola. His father was a silk merchant who died when Daniel was ten. Soon after, his mother converted to Calvinism and moved with her son to the northern Netherlands. Several years later he began paint-ing and in 1611 he moved back to Antwerp. He studied with Jan Brueghel the Elder and associated with the artistic circle that formed around Peter Paul Rubens, one of the artistic geniuses of that epoch.

After his return to Flanders, Seghers rejoined the Catholic Church and in 1614 he entered the Society of Jesus as a lay brother. After his two-year novitiate in Rome, he returned to Antwerp and devoted himself to the ministry of religious painting. Although he refused to sell his works, the Jesuits would give them as gifts to various churches, monas-teries, and wealthy individual art lovers, including several princes and dukes. He became known throughout Europe for paintings that featured fabulous garlands of flowers encompassing sacred scenes or saints, a style that reflects the profound influence of Ignatian contemplation and, in particular, the use of the imagination in the composition of place. Seghers worked as an artist until his death in 1661.

Daniel Seghers' mysterious *Madonna and Child with Garlands* is more than a beautiful painting on a religious theme: it is a visual Ignatian contemplation.[1] The astonishing realism of the floral bouquet—brilliant with color and variety and attended by an angelic host of butterflies—arrests the eye and draws the believer into contemplation. The act of seeing the composition launches the beholder into the borderland of contrasts between light and darkness, immediacy and remoteness, warmth and coolness, vibrancy and tranquility, sensory experience and mystical intuition. One not only sees Seghers' florid colors and balanced forms, one feels his dramatic energy, smells his Edenic blossoms, and

Madonna and Child with Garlands by Daniel Seghers, s.j. Photo-Reproduction

hears the astonishing silence of his cathedral-like composition. One *enters* this painting in the same way that one enters Ignatian prayer, particularly the exercise of the Second Week that is commonly called the "application of the senses" (121–26).

Ignatian contemplatives seek God *in the world*. Ignatian artists like Daniel Seghers perceive God's presence in the *concrete details* of the world such as the particular flowers in this painting. It is crucial, however, to note that, for all their beauty, Seghers' garlands are not the heart of the mystery. They function almost like a window, leading the viewer beyond the garland's dense beauty into the presence of the One who created every flower. And the genius of Seghers appears precisely in this: *viewers do not immediately perceive the heart of this painting*. To see its heart we have to step forward, to draw near. We have to peer through the wreath as though peering through a window. In this act of concentrated seeing we discover the amazing, almost pristine mystery at the very center of the painting: the human mother holding her divine child.

Seghers' *Madonna and Child with Garlands* functions as a visual contemplation on the incarnation. In the fifth contemplation dedicated to this theme (the so-called application of the senses), Ignatius tells the director that "it is profitable to use the imagination and to apply the five senses" (SpEx 121) to the subject matter of the incarnation (101–17). The director should lead the exercitant to be able to say: "By the sight of my imagination I will see the persons" (122), "By my hearing I will listen to what they are saying" (123), "I will smell the fragrance and taste the infinite sweetness and charm of the Divinity" (124), to "embrace and kiss the places where the persons walk or sit" (125), all in order to go beyond these details to *the more*, the heart of the mystery itself.

The Ignatian pedagogy implicit in Seghers' masterpiece teaches us to draw near and find *in* this place—this world where Christ becomes incarnate—that Christ is indeed incarnate and present still. The mystery is here, now. It is the mystery that the world's savior has come into the world as a tiny human infant, that the one who holds the world is held in and by the world. It is the mystery that our world is itself the object of God's compassionate gaze. The color, rhythm, and vitality of this world spring from the hand of the Divine Artist, the one who painted creation into being. "Here," the human artist seems to say, "is a cause for wonder, reverence, and praise"—movements of the spirit that embody the very heart of Ignatian prayer.

Kevin F. Burke, s.j.

Gerard Manley Hopkins (1844–1889)

Gerard Manley Hopkins was an English Jesuit whose poetry, most of which was published posthumously, places him among the greatest poets writing during the Victorian age.[1] The oldest of nine children born to Anglican parents, he converted to Catholicism at the age of twenty-two and shortly thereafter entered the Society of Jesus. His career was largely unspectacular. He worked in parish ministry and taught at various schools in England and Ireland, but partly due to poor physical health he suffered from fierce bouts of depression and melancholy. He died at the age of forty-four of typhoid fever.

On the surface Hopkins' life appears dreary and tragic. Unbeknownst to all but a few close friends, however, he possessed a profound ability to apprehend the deep interconnections among things and to render those interconnections in compact poetic language. His letters, homilies, and personal papers contain insightful and original contributions to literary criticism. Early in his career he coined the term "inscape" to refer to the particularity inherent in every unique thing:

> Each mortal thing does one thing and the same:
> Deals out that being indoors each one dwells;
> Selves—goes itself; *myself* it speaks and spells,
> Crying *Whát I do is me: for that I came.*

Hopkins' notebooks testify that, through patient observation, he sought to recognize the inscape, the particularity, of every individual object he encountered. His poetry witnesses that, under the impact of the imagination and through the miracle of language, he aimed to bring this "selfness" to articulation. Later on, during his Jesuit studies, he encountered the thought of the great medieval philosopher, Duns Scotus; there he discovered a philosophical framework to support this penetrating aes-

104

thetic intuition. Even more important, under the impact of the Ignatian Exercises, he mastered a spirituality of contemplative praxis that corresponded beautifully to his fundamental poetic intuitions.

But it was his poems themselves that helped to inaugurate an epochal shift in English literary history, even though the corpus of his finished poems is relatively spare and they were only discovered and published decades after his death. Hopkins revolutionized the way we scan and hear poetic lines. His subtle rhyme schemes and uncanny rhythms—including the invention of what he called "sprung rhythm"— along with his passionate realism, powers of observation, and poignant faith find voice in a stunning array of images quarried from nature as well as from the harrowing cliffs of personal desolation and spiritual crisis. All of this can be detected in the selections to follow. Additionally, these poems testify to the indelible link between his poetic genius and spiritual depth. Indeed, one might say that in Hopkins, the poetry of inscape and Ignatian spirituality are one.

Hopkins' poems—compact, charged with color, sprung from the depths of religious human experience—are themselves each unique. For this reason they cannot be easily categorized. At the same time, certain themes surface again and again within his poems. Thus, for example, in the ten poems collected here one notices the frequent appearances of the Ignatian dyad of consolation and desolation.

The first five poems breathe with the consolation that attends the experience of "finding God in all things." The descriptions are vivid and concrete, appealing to every sense both in the rhythmic structures and imaginative contents of the poems. Here, Hopkins contemplates the trinitarian God attending to his creation and filling it with divine dignity. Graced encounters with passing earthly beauty evoke genuine reverence for the One *whose beauty is past change* ("Pied Beauty"). Indeed, Hopkins exclaims, *The world is charged with the grandeur of God* ("God's Grandeur") and for that very reason he is able to *lift up heart, eyes, down all that glory in the heavens to glean our Saviour* ("Hurrahing in Harvest"). Likewise, Hopkins finds Christ who *plays in ten thousand places* ("As kingfishers catch fire") through the inscape of the *dapple-dawn-drawn Falcon* ("The Windhover"). Finally, he notes in wonder that *the Holy Ghost over the bent world broods with warm breast and with ah! bright wings* ("God's Grandeur").

The latter five poems include three preeminent examples of what critics call the "terrible sonnets." In these poems we see Hopkins battling against *despair* while *wrestling with God* ("Carrion Comfort"). We feel his *grief, gall,* and *heartburn* ("I wake and feel the fell of dark"), his sense of spiritual abandonment, his *tormented mind tormenting yet* ("My own heart let me more have pity on"). In all of this, we encounter a shocking, furious self-loathing that rivals the worst moments of Loyola in the cave at Manresa. But spiritual desolation does not signal the end of hope, even though it might feel hopeless. Despite—or even because of—the internal oppression Hopkins tellingly calls *the fell of dark*, he is driven to prayer. This drive, this impulse to pray, appears explicitly in the poem "Thou art indeed just, Lord," where Hopkins the poet, like Jeremiah the prophet, like Job, and above all like Jesus, bows in the end before the mystery of God, uttering a most plaintive and poignant prayer: *Mine, O thou lord of life, send my roots rain.* Likewise, we encounter his reverence for the hidden workings of God's grace in the ordinary life of an extraordinary mystic, the Spanish Jesuit, "St. Alphonsus Rodriguez."

Kevin F. Burke, s.j.

From *The Poems of Gerard Manley Hopkins*[2]

1. Pied Beauty

Glory be to God for dappled things—
    For skies of couple-colour as a brinded cow;
        For rose-moles all in stipple upon trout that swim;
Fresh-firecoal chestnut-falls; finches' wings;
    Landscape plotted and pieced—fold, fallow, and plough;
        And áll trádes, their gear and tackle and trim.
All things counter, original, spare, strange;
    Whatever is fickle, freckled (who knows how?)
        With swift, slow; sweet, sour; adazzle, dim;
He fathers-forth whose beauty is past change:
        Praise him.

2. God's Grandeur

The world is charged with the grandeur of God.
    It will flame out, like shining from shook foil;
    It gathers to a greatness, like the ooze of oil
Crushed. Why do men then now not reck his rod?
Generations have trod, have trod, have trod;
    And all is seared with trade; bleared, smeared with toil;
    And wears man's smudge and shares man's smell: the soil
Is bare now, nor can foot feel, being shod.

And for all this, nature is never spent;
　　There lives the dearest freshness deep down things;
And though the last lights off the black West went
　　Oh, morning, at the brown brink eastward, springs—
Because the Holy Ghost over the bent
　　World broods with warm breast and with ah! bright wings.

3. *The Windhover:*
To Christ our Lord

I caught this morning morning's minion, kingdom of
　　daylight's dauphin, dapple-dawn-drawn Falcon, in his riding
　　Of the rolling level underneath him steady air, and striding
High there, how he rung upon the rein of a wimpling wing
In his ecstasy! then off, off forth on swing,
　　As a skate's heel sweeps smooth on a bow-bend: the hurl
　　　　and gliding
　　Rebuffed the big wind. My heart in hiding
Stirred for a bird,—the achieve of; the mastery of the thing!

Brute beauty and valour and act, oh, air, pride, plume, here
　　Buckle! AND the fire that breaks from thee then, a billion
Times told lovelier, more dangerous, O my chevalier!
　　No wonder of it: shéer plód makes plough down sillion
Shine, and blue-bleak embers, ah my dear,
　　Fall, gall themselves, and gash gold-vermillion.

4. (*As kingfishers catch fire, dragonflies dráw fláme*)

As kingfishers catch fire, dragonflies dráw fláme;
As tumbled over rim in roundy wells
Stones ring; like each tucked string tells, each hung bell's
Bow swung finds tongue to fling out broad its name;
Each mortal thing does one thing and the same:
Deals out that being indoors each one dwells;
Selves—goes itself; *myself* it speaks and spells,
Crying *Whát I do is me: for that I came.*

Í say móre: the just man justices;
Kéeps gráce: thát keeps all his goings graces;
Acts in God's eye what in God's eye he is—
Chríst—for Christ plays in ten thousand places,
Lovely in limbs, and lovely in eyes not his
To the Father through the features of men's faces.

5. Hurrahing in Harvest

Summer ends now; now, barbarous in beauty, the stooks arise
    Around; up above, what wind-walks! what lovely behaviour
    Of silk-sack clouds! has wilder, wilful-wavier
Meal-drift moulded ever and melted across skies?

I walk, I lift up, I lift up heart, eyes,
    Down all that glory in the heavens to glean our Saviour;
    And, éyes, heárt, what looks, what lips yet gave you a
Rapturous love's greeting of realer, of rounder replies?

And the azurous hung hills are his world-wielding shoulder
    Majestic—as a stallion stalwart, very-violet-sweet!—
These things, these things were here and but the beholder
    Wanting; which two when they once meet,
The heart rears wings bold and bolder
    And hurls for him, O half hurls earth for him off under his feet.

6. (Carrion Comfort)

Not, I'll not, carrion comfort, Despair, not feast on thee;
Not untwist—slack they may be—these last strands of man
In me ór, most weary, cry *I can no more*. I can;
Can something, hope, wish day come, not choose not to be.
But ah, but O thou terrible, why wouldst thou rude on me
Thy wring-world right foot rock? lay a lionlimb against me? scan
With darksome devouring eyes my bruisèd bones? and fan,
O in turns of tempest, me heaped there; me frantic to avoid thee
      and flee?

    Why? That my chaff might fly; my grain lie, sheer and clear.
Nay in all that toil, that coil, since (seems) I kissed the rod,
Hand rather, my heart lo! lapped strength, stole joy, would laugh, chéer.
Cheer whom though? the hero whose heaven-handling flung me,
      fóot tród
Me? or me that fought him? O which one? is it each one? That
      night, that year
Of now done darkness I wretch lay wrestling with (my God!) my God.

7. (I wake and feel the fell of dark, not day)

I wake and feel the fell of dark, not day.
What hours, O what black hoürs we have spent
This night! what sights you, heart, saw; ways you went!

And more must, in yet longer light's delay.
    With witness I speak this. But where I say
Hours I mean years, mean life. And my lament
Is cries countless, cries like dead letters sent
To dearest him that lives alas! away.

    I am gall, I am heartburn. God's most deep decree
Bitter would have me taste: my taste was me;
Bones built in me, flesh filled, blood brimmed the curse.
    Selfyeast of spirit a dull dough sours. I see
The lost are like this, and their scourge to be
As I am mine, their sweating selves; but worse.

8. *(My own heart let me more have pity on)*

My own heart let me more have pity on; let
Me live to my sad self hereafter kind,
Charitable; not live this tormented mind
With this tormented mind tormenting yet.
    I cast for comfort I can no more get
By groping round my comfortless, than blind
Eyes in their dark can day or thirst can find
Thirst 's all-in-all in all a world of wet.

Soul, self; come, poor Jackself, I do advise
You, jaded, let be; call off thoughts awhile
Elsewhere; leave comfort root-room; let joy size
At God knows when to God knows what; whose smile
's not wrung, see you; unforeseen times rather—as skies
Betweenpie mountains—lights a lovely mile.

9. *(Thou art indeed just, Lord)*

Justus quidem tu es, Domine, si disputem tecum:
    verumtamen justa loquar ad te:
Quare via impiorum prosperatur? &c.

Thou art indeed just, Lord, if I contend
With thee; but, sir, so what I plead is just.
Why do sinners' ways prosper? and why must
Disappointment all I endeavour end?
    Wert thou my enemy, O thou my friend,
How wouldst thou worse, I wonder, than thou dost
Defeat, thwart me? Oh, the sots and thralls of lust
Do in spare hours more thrive than I that spend,

Sir, life upon thy cause. See, banks and brakes
Now leavèd how thick! lacèd they are again
With fretty chervil, look, and fresh wind shakes
Them; birds build—but not I build; no, but strain,
Time's eunuch, and not breed one work that wakes.
Mine, O thou lord of life, send my roots rain.

10. In honour of
St. Alphonsus Rodriguez
Laybrother of the Society of Jesus

Honour is flashed off exploit, so we say;
And those strokes once that gashed flesh or galled shield
Should tongue that time now, trumpet now that field,
And, on the fighter, forge his glorious day.
On Christ they do and on the martyr may;
But be the war within, the brand we wield
Unseen, the heroic breast not outward-steeled,
Earth hears no hurtle then from fiercest fray.

Yet God (that hews mountain and continent,
Earth, all, out; who, with trickling increment,
Veins violets and tall trees makes more and more)
Could crowd career with conquest while there went
Those years and years by of world without event
That in Majorca Alfonso watched the door.

William F. Lynch (1908–1987)

Born in New York City to an Irish immigrant family, William Lynch emerged in the middle of the twentieth century as a champion of both the classics and the modern secular world, of the imagination as passage to the real, and of the human city in a time of polarization and brazen inhumanity.[1] His home city shaped him and supplied many of the concrete images with which he promoted the vocation of "building the human city." But New York City was not a fortress for Lynch. Indeed, his love for his native city was interwoven with his fascination with harbor rivers (like the East River) that flow through the city to the sea, connecting the city to the rest of the world. In a late and unusually auto-biographical essay entitled "Me and the East River," Lynch revealed what crucial symbols like rivers provide: "What does this dirty river give? It gives us a world. . . . We need such a world. Of all the things we need, we need a world."[2]

It is significant to note that nearly all of Lynch's writings are concerned with images, imagination, and sensibility, above all with a realistic imagi-nation and an integrating sensibility. At the same time, the range of his concrete interests is vast. For this reason it is hard to know exactly what to call him. Philosopher, theologian, literary and dramatic critic, scholar of the psychological, the social, the political, and the spiritual, and cham-pion of everyday life and ordinary people: Lynch was all these and more. He was, in a certain sense, utterly unique as a thinker, a public intellectual (in the best sense of the word) as well as a highly refined reader of classical and contemporary artists, dramatists, and theorists. If we refer to him as a literary critic, the label should not be taken in a narrow or superficial sense. He was a philosopher of the dramatic human condition lived in time, finitude, and hope. He was, finally, a Christian philosopher in the fullest sense of the word.

111

Lynch was also Catholic through and through, though not in a doc-trinaire or narrowly denominational sense. A brilliant student and scholar, he ranged over the entire terrain of human thought, yet chafed against the rigidity and lack of imagination that dominated Catholic intellectual life (and his own Jesuit formation) in the decades following the modernist crisis. In contrast to a defensive and formulaic version of Catholicism, Lynch was "catholic" above all for the way that he resisted contemporary versions of a "gnostic" or Manichean sensibility and various forms of what he calls the "absolutizing instinct." He was "catholic" in the way he sought "both/and" solutions to dilemmas hopelessly cast in polarized, "either/or" terms. Years after his death his writings retain a freshness imbued with a Catholic sacramental imagination seeking ever to relate spirit to body and to find a world for the human. "I am intent on creating, and in a very imaginable way, a body for faith and, very specially, a political and social embodiment of faith."

Having graduated from Regis High School and Fordham University in New York, Lynch entered the Jesuits at the age of 26 (a "delayed voca-tion" in an era when most Jesuit novices entered directly out of high school). Because he had already completed a college degree before he entered the Jesuits, he pursued a doctorate in classics prior to his theo-logical studies. After his ordination in 1945 he returned to Fordham to teach and in 1950 he became the editor of *Thought* magazine. Like Hopkins, however, Lynch suffered from bouts with depression. He endured at least one serious episode that required hospitalization for some weeks in 1956. On the basis of this difficult experience he later wrote one of his most important and widely read books, *Images of Hope: Imagination as Healer of the Hopeless* (1965).

Between 1957 and 1962 Lynch taught English at Georgetown Univer-sity, a period during which he published four major books, including another of his best-known works, *Christ and Apollo: The Dimensions of the Literary Imagination* (1960). He was featured in an article in the May 23, 1960, issue of *Time* magazine and was called "one of the most incisive Catholic intellectuals in the U.S." After 1962 Lynch worked as a writer-in-residence at St. Peter's College in New Jersey. He won the National Catholic Book Award in 1970 for his book, *Christ and Prometheus: A New Image of the Secular* and in 1973 published a brilliant meditation modeled on Pascal's *Pensées* entitled *Images of Faith: An Exploration of the Ironic Imagi-nation* (1973). Lynch died of leukemia in New York at the age of 78.

We have chosen from his books a limited number of brief quotations and divided them into three sections. The first, "Imagining a Body for

Faith," opens with a selection from *Images of Faith*. It focuses on "the concrete movement of faith and the imagination through the definite, through the human, through the actual life of Christ." In this it serves, as he himself notes, as a summary of everything he wrote. Brief selections from two other major works underscore the importance Lynch assigns to the imagination and the images it creates. The stakes are high. "We can make or destroy the world with an image."

The second section, "Into the Valley of the Human," presents selections from Lynch's best-known and perhaps most widely admired work, *Images of Hope*. He explores the "absolutizing instinct" that underlies contemporary forms of Gnosticism and illuminates the way this instinct produces a sense of "hopelessness" that can only be ameliorated through the ministrations of the "concrete imagination." Significantly, too, he analyzes how hope depends on help and the freedom to seek help when one is in trouble.

The final selection, "The *Spiritual Exercises* and the Definite," comes from another of Lynch's most successful and popular works, *Christ and Apollo*. Like Hopkins and Seghers, Lynch gives special attention to the Ignatian composition of place and the role of the imagination in the practice of faith. He also explores the way the Spiritual Exercises lead one step-by-step into and through the world. Saint Ignatius, Lynch argues, never allows us to escape finitude or magically leap beyond time. Rather, he insists that disciples follow Christ in the world so as to find God there. Underlining this crucial theme, Lynch illuminates the brilliant though counterintuitive way the Ignatian Exercises lead us to embrace our human condition as a blessing, not a curse.

Kevin F. Burke, s.j.

Imagining a Body for Faith (From *Images of Faith, Images of Hope*, and *Christ and Prometheus*)

I am intent on creating, and in a very imaginable way, a body for faith and, very specially, a political and social embodiment of faith. How much shall we imagine that body and still remain religious thinkers or imaginers? This is not an idle or a passing question. In fact, I am sure that there are many who will say that it happens to be precisely the central question of modern theology; it creates a threatening division between two great groups among Christians today. The activist, the radical, and the revolutionary tend to say that the detail of the metaphor and its location in experience is the whole of the matter; the other half of the polarity tends to see this as an attack on the true religion of the living God.

Just like talk about God, *this* contemporary tendency to schism cannot be settled by one aphorism or cheap slogan but must be come at in a number of ways. If I may give a rough description of where I stand I repeat that everything I have ever written asks for the concrete movement of faith and the imagination through experience, through time, through the definite, through the human, through the actual life of Christ. . . . There is all the difference in the world between saying that faith must have a political embodiment and saying that this means [people] of faith have the final political answers. . . . We do need and must have activism, we can no longer accept passivity, but it will be the irony of faith itself that can alone prevent the revolution from falling, ironically, into a new clericalism and a religious fascism that will listen to no word in assembly but its own.[3]

***

One of the permanent meanings of imagination has been that it is the gift that envisions what cannot yet be seen, the gift that constantly proposes to itself that the boundaries of the possible are wider than they seem. Imagination, if it is in prison and has tried every exit, does not panic or move into apathy but sits down to try to envision another way out. It is always slow to admit that all the facts are in, that all the doors have been tried, and that it is defeated. It is not so much that it has vision as that it is able to wait, to wait for a moment of vision which is not yet there, for a door that is not yet locked. It is not overcome by the absoluteness of the present moment.[4]

***

The imagination is not an aesthetic faculty. It is not a single or special faculty. It is all the resources of [a person], all his faculties, his whole history, his whole life, and his whole heritage, all brought to bear upon the concrete world inside and outside of himself, to form images of the world, and thus to find it, cope with it, shape it, even make it. The task of the imagination is to imagine the real. However, that might also very well mean making the real, making the world, for every image formed by everybody is an active, creative step, for good or for bad. . . .

The imagination is really the only way we have of handling the world. It is at the point of the imagination, at the precise point where an image is formed, that we meet the world, deal with it, judge it.

If the imagination is the whole of us struggling, through images, with the world, then our images are not the innocent, purely objective things they seem to be. The most casual image contains the whole of human being. Images are not snapshots of reality. They are what we have made of reality. Everything in us pours into the simplest image. They are ourselves. . . .

All of our principal and habitual images have an extraordinary range and content that only emerges into awareness under analysis or in a period of emergency. This is true of the image we have of a man, a woman, a child, birth, life, death, morning, night, food, friend, the enemy, the self, the human, the world as world, the secular world that immediately surrounds us. These images are packed with experience, history, concepts, judgments, decisions, wishes, hopes, disappointments, love, and hate. And all this gets into the actual concrete visible, audible, tactile stuff of our images. Thus one cannot get closer to a man, nor can a man get closer to himself, than through his images. They not only come at us from the world; we also come at the world through them, in love or hate. We can make or destroy the world with an image.[5]

Into the Valley of the Human (From *Images of Hope*)

As I see it, we are always faced with programmatic alternatives:

We can decide to build a human city, a city of man, in which all men have citizenship, Greek, Jew, and Gentile, the black and the white, the maimed, the halt, and the blind, the mentally well and the mentally ill. This will always require an act of the imagination which will extend the idea of the human and which will imagine nothing in man it cannot contain. The idea of the human and the idea of the city of man will have to remain eternally open and flexible, ready to adjust itself to the new, to new races, and, above all, to new illnesses. How many men are up to the building of this kind of city remains to be seen. . . .

Or we will decide to build various absolute and walled cities, from which various pockets of our humanity will always be excluded. They will pose as ideal cities, and will exclude the imagination, the Negro, the sick, the different. These totalistic, these non-human cities offer an extraordinary fascination for the souls of fearful men and we are fools if we underestimate how strong and seductive they can be. . . . Whatever form these non-human cities take they will always have to be self-enclosed, will always have their own defenses, and their own weapons. The citizens spend their time reassuring each other and hating everyone else. Actually they will never be safe and the final irony will be that they will have to make war on each other. Only the city of the human would have been safe. . . .

Our subjects indeed are hope and hopelessness; but it will turn out that one of the great hopes of all men is that they shall be human and belong to the city of man—and one of the great sources of our hopelessness will come from these rigid and absolutized, these non-human constructions that lead to the self-enclosure of despair. . . .

It is impossible to break hope if it chooses not to be broken. But that is no excuse for placing impossible and hopeless burdens upon it.

The first of these burdens—all of them the creation of an absolutizing tendency in [human beings]—would be to declare that hope is a final interior resource, which needs nothing but itself. The sick, who have never been asked, know that this is absolute nonsense.

The fact is that hope is a relative idea. It is always relative to the idea of help. It seeks help. It depends. It looks to the outside world. There are no absolute heroes. That is not the way hope works. The absolute heroes are afraid of help. But hope is not. . . .

Hope comes close to being the very heart and center of a human being. It is the best resource of [a person], always there on the inside, making everything possible when he is in action, or waiting to be illuminated when he is ill. It is his most inward possession, and is rightly thought of, according to the Pandora story, as still there when everything else has gone.

But it would be an intolerable burden for the well or the mentally ill if hope turned out to be a rigidly and exclusively interior thing. The sick, who have reached the limit of their interior resources, are often told to hold on to this completely inward kind of romantic hope. There is a whole literature of such eloquent rhetoric. It speaks endlessly of the absolute and interior spark in man that cannot be overcome and that needs nothing but itself. I shall discuss some of its concrete forms. Medically or spiritually it is nonsense and harmful—especially to the sick when they are told it is there and they know it really is not.

If we did not know that hope is a relative idea, related to the outside world and to help, we would all become sick or sicker than we are. Hope is a deeply relative idea. The well hope for a response from the world, whether they are breathing or working or in love. If the response is not there, trouble starts. With the ill, there is less relationship, less call, less response, more fear of help or response when it is there, and therefore far more trouble. Hope, since it is not in every sense an absolute, must rediscover the other half of itself, the outside world and the idea of help.

Thus we analyze and attack a first form of the absolutizing instinct. . . .

By the absolutizing instinct, I mean something very literal and nothing complicated. I mean the instinct in human beings that tends to absolutize everything, to make an absolute out of everything it touches. . . .

The absolutizing instinct magnifies. In its presence each thing loses its true perspective and its true edges. The good becomes the tremendously good, the evil becomes the absolutely evil, the grey becomes the black or white, the complicated, because it is difficult to handle, becomes, in desperation, the completely simple. The small becomes the big.

But above all, everything assumes a greater weight than it has and becomes a greater burden. I wish to emphasize this quality of weight in everything that comes from the operation of the absolutizing instinct, and I want to forewarn about the burden it makes of everything. The absolutizing instinct is the father of the hopeless and adds that special feeling of weight that hopelessness attaches to everything it touches. It is, in general, the creator of hopeless projects and the creator of idols.

According to the stricter terms of the vocabulary I am using . . . the absolutizing instinct is not really an action of the imagination. Rather, it is a creator of fantasy, distortion, magnification; it is invariably in full and violent operation before it ever meets its object and by the time it is finished nothing much is left of the object's boundaries or edges or identity. The object has been elevated to the status of a dream and has lost its own name. This instinct is a maker of dreams and does not give a tinker's dam for objects or people. . . .

Some medical [people] would say that learning to tolerate ambivalence is a decisive struggle for the sick in their conquest of hopelessness. Such a position tallies remarkably, though analogically, with the findings and the goals of true religion. . . .

The process of healing by making ambivalence possible is an agonizing one. [People] set their hearts on love, on love pure and simple and absolute. Now, it *seems*, they must watch it turn to hate, must see it as a corruptible and corrupting thing. The myth of the absolute is being exploded, and the absolutizing part of us is in despair. All will be well in the end, however, because love will be recognized as love, and hate as hate, while each will prevent the other from becoming an infinite frightening giant. The path to this ambivalence is through hopelessness to hope. Because, when it is surmounted and accepted, the sick leave the nightmare world of unqualified, absolute feelings to revel in the valley of the human. It is a valley of peace guarded by a purgatory of fire.[6]

The *Spiritual Exercises* and the Definite (From *Christ and Apollo*)

I should like to propose the *Spiritual Exercises* of St. Ignatius as a source of poetic as well as spiritual insight . . . into the image of the definite and the image of time, for he has much to say about both.

Certainly [Ignatius] wished to lead the soul to God, and if people wish to call that escape they are at times entitled to the use of their own words. But his method was not the method of escape or magic. Magical or instantaneous methods of getting at God are marked by a hatred and fear of human time and of the full, long human process. Basically they wish to do two things—and I want to lay strong emphasis on this because both contrast strongly with the Ignatian method of coming to God; because of this hatred of time they wish to use but a single, special moment of it, one that by some strange, inexplicable "trick" will lead them to full glory, and they wish to deprive even that single moment of as much of its highly questionable actuality and concreteness as possible, thinking that these are blocks to the cognition of glory and beauty. Ignatius, thoroughly representative of Catholic theology, works entirely in the contrary direction. An analysis of his method will show in detail after detail that, as a seeker of God, he is completely devoted to the time process and completely devoted to its definite actuality, no matter what it is at each particular moment. Therefore his method of prayer or, shall we say, his directive for leading the soul to God, has two main structural points behind it:

1. He leads the exercitant, the [person] making the exercises, *proportionally* through the life of Christ. Therefore, he leads him

through it step by step, forbidding him again and again to take the way of magic impatience or hatred and commanding him to stay within the pure time process as such. It is hoped that the texts which are used later will make perfectly clear what is meant by this.

2. He is remarkably definite in his demands on the soul that the latter be altogether concrete in its consideration of that moment of time. This is that point of his technique and, we should also say, of his *theology* which is called the "composition of place." In it he insists that the one praying should submit his mind and will completely to perfect and complete *detail*, the detail of that moment which is being separately and patiently considered. Once again I hope that the naked texts will reveal precisely what he meant, and in their complete simplicity. For nothing could be simpler and barer in their style, save a mathematical treatise, than the *Spiritual Exercises*. It is only the impassioned and actual quality of the theology behind them which reveals the high and thoughtful life behind these few bare pages.

But we must remember that it is exactly through such proportional and definite methods that he wishes to lead the soul to God and beauty, and that that is his only and ever-recurrent theme. In his method he is completely human, time-possessed and definite. . . .

Thus, then, we have an extraordinary and at times disconcerting document which combines, in unified and sharp strokes, time, detail, definiteness, actuality, and glory.[7]

PART VII
RENEWAL

In 1935, in anticipation of the fourth centenary of the founding of the Society of Jesus, Superior General Wlodimir Ledochowski convened a group of Jesuit scholars in Rome to assess the history and current practice of the order's spirituality. It was a risky time to pursue such a review. The world surrounding the Catholic Church was bubbling with wars and rumors of wars. Within the church itself, powerful, anti-Enlightenment elements bristled against the *nouvelle theologie* despite the fact that this "new theology" sprang from a return to more ancient sources. Precisely in this context, led by Joseph de Guibert, a French theologian teaching at the Gregorian University in Rome, the Society of Jesus inaugurated a retrieval of Ignatian sources and a renewal of Ignatian spiritual life that continues to this day.

Part 7 of *The Ignatian Tradition* scans this astonishing renewal of Ignatian spirituality. No other time in the last five hundred years has seen such a torrent of study focused on the movement begun by Ignatius and his followers. No other period allowed such an explosion of innovation and experimentation in Ignatian spiritual practice. Viewed within the context of Vatican II and its call for the renewal of the church's scriptural understanding, liturgical custom, doctrinal formulation, ethical practice, and devotional life, the renewal of the Ignatian tradition can be counted as one of the great blessings of the council's *aggiornamento*. The final four chapters of this study concentrate on several among the many figures who enacted this graced renewal of Ignatian spirituality: Pedro Arrupe, the superior general elected near the end of Vatican II who directed the Society's response to the council; George Ganss, a scholar who continued the work begun by de Guibert;

121

Josée Gsell, a French laywoman who led the renewal of a key Ignatian lay movement; and the corporate voice of the Society's General Congregations 32 and 34.

Eileen Burke-Sullivan

Pedro Arrupe (1907–1991)

No single follower of the Ignatian tradition can be given greater credit for the dramatic renewal of the spirituality in the twentieth century than the second Basque to be elected general of the Society of Jesus, Pedro Arrupe. Born in Bilbao, Spain, in 1907 to a family of modest means, he lost his mother when he was ten and his father when he was eighteen. The youngest child and only son, Arrupe initially pursued medical studies at the University of Madrid. During a visit to Lourdes with his sisters he witnessed miraculous healings, which led him to reorder his plans and enter the Jesuits in 1927.

In 1932 when all the Jesuits were expelled from Spain, Arrupe went into exile in Belgium. For several months he had no official assignment, so he began reading the letters, mission histories, and memoirs of Jesuits from the time of Ignatius down to the present day contained in approximately 125 volumes of the *Monumenta Historica Societatis Jesu*. Arrupe "caught" the spirit of the early Jesuits in their own words and in terms of their concrete experiences. This had enormous implications later when, as general, he led the Society's renewal: his appropriation of the Ignatian vision depended not on some grand theory but from having watched it develop step by gradual step through the lives of actual Jesuits.

Arrupe's own life continued to unfold step-by-step in the context of the extraordinary events of his own day. On the eve of the Second World War his superiors sent him to Japan as a missionary. Just after the bombing of Pearl Harbor he was arrested and held in solitary confinement for thirty-three days by the Japanese government, which suspected him of espionage. Shortly after his release from prison in 1942, Arrupe went to Nagatsuka on the outskirts of Hiroshima to become the master of novices. On the morning of August 6, 1945, when the first atomic bomb virtually incinerated Hiroshima, Arrupe and his novices converted their home into a makeshift hospital. Drawing on his earlier medical training, he treated over 150 people suffering from the mysterious aftereffects of radiation poisoning. This apocalyptic event changed his life. It deepened his sense of dependence on God and opened his eyes to "what is deadly and truly terrible about force and violence."[1]

In October 1964, Arrupe traveled to Rome as a delegate to General Congregation 31 to help elect the successor to the recently deceased superior general, Jean-Baptiste Janssens. On the morning of May 22, 1965, the Congregation elected him. As an immediate consequence of his election, he received an invitation to participate in the final session of Vatican II. He advised the bishops on the signs of the times and the importance of inculturation, two crucial themes in the Pastoral Constitution on the Church in the Modern World.

In the period of renewal following Vatican II Arrupe embodied a view of religious leadership rooted in collegiality, discernment, and service. In response to the conciliar decree on religious life he promoted an intensive updating of the Society of Jesus in view of its original Ignatian charism. He encouraged the scholarly study of the sources of Jesuit religious life along with a renewed practice of the Spiritual Exercises. This had an immediate impact on the Society; indeed many historians viewed it as nothing short of a refounding of the order.

But Arrupe's influence went far beyond the Society of Jesus. He served as the president of the Union of Religious Superiors General for fifteen years. In this capacity he regularly attended bishops' meetings and synods and represented the many religious communities with whom he consulted and advised. He particularly nurtured renewal of women's religious communities founded in the Ignatian tradition and strongly supported a thoroughgoing renewal in Ignatian spirituality and life practice for the lay movement of the Sodality (Congregation of Mary), which was a Jesuit mission.

Arrupe's personal concern for the poor and his visionary reading of the church's social gospel fed his concern to renew the vitality of Christian discipleship around the intrinsic connection between faith and justice. This became the defining mark of his years as the general of the Society of Jesus.

On September 7, 1981, still serving as general of the Society of Jesus, Arrupe suffered a massive stroke from which he never fully recovered. His resignation was finally accepted at General Congregation 33 called in 1983. After another eight years of suffering he died quietly in Rome in 1991. While physically small, like Ignatius himself, Pedro Arrupe is one of the spiritual giants of the twentieth century. As a man of deep prayer, devotion, and discipline, as an able administrator, teacher, writer, public speaker, and priest, he redefined for our day the Ignatian vocation of the contemplative in action.

Pedro Arrupe's corpus of writing available in English includes nine collections of essays, instructions, letters, informal talks, formal addresses, homilies, interviews, and memoirs, only a few of which we are able to reproduce here. The first selection comes from a section of a major essay Arrupe wrote in 1980 titled "The Trinitarian Inspiration of the Ignatian Charism." In this excerpt he analyzes Ignatius' crucial mystical experience at La Storta. The second selection comes from one of Arrupe's most famous addresses, "Men and Women for Others." Originally titled "Men for Others" but later emended by Arrupe himself, this address was given to a gathering of alumni of Jesuit schools in Europe in 1973. The phrase "Men and Women for Others" now serves as an unofficial motto for a variety of schools and service agencies that operate under the Ignatian inspiration. The final section, "Love for Christ Poor," includes five brief excerpts taken from a variety of sources. These selections witness to the importance Arrupe gave to the poor. At the same time they aptly place love at the very heart of the Ignatian charism.

Eileen Burke-Sullivan and Kevin F. Burke, s.j.

From "The Trinitarian Inspiration of the Ignatian Charism"

La Storta is a place 17 kilometers from Rome, where a small chapel stands at the intersection of the ancient Roman road along which they were coming and a lateral road. Ignatius, with [Diego] Laínez and [Pierre] Favre, entered the village *"and making a prayer, felt such a change coming over his soul and saw so clearly that God the Father was placing him with Christ his Son that he could not doubt that God the Father was indeed placing him with his Son."* This is the sum total of what we know about the event that Ignatius will recount 18 years later.

But Laínez, who was present and no doubt received immediate and detailed confidences, has spelled out for us the content of that illumination, which could not have more far-reaching consequences. And Ignatius has stated that *"all that Laínez said was true."* What Laínez said and later wrote was this: Ignatius was singularly favored by spiritual feelings all during the trip from Vicenza to La Storta, especially when he would receive communion from the hand of Favre or Laínez himself. He had the sensation at La Storta that the Father was impressing these words on his heart: I will be propitious to you in Rome. On the occasion we are referring to, Ignatius felt he could *"see Christ with his cross on his shoulder, and together with him the Father, who was telling him: I want you to serve us. For this reason, Ignatius, taking great devotion from that most holy name, wanted the congregation to be called the Society of Jesus"* [Laínez].

The profound meaning of this enlightenment is very clear: the Divine Persons accept him into their service. It is the divine confirmation that Ignatius wanted at that crucial moment of his life. The generic call of the Cardoner is now explicitly and formally restated. Just as had happened at the time of "that so great illumination," the habitual low-key Ignatian prose style bursts into flame: *"he felt such a change coming over his soul and saw so vividly."*[2]

From "Men and Women for Others"

The Men and Women the Church Needs Today

What kind of man or woman is needed today by the Church, by the world? One who is a "man-or-woman-for-others." That is my shorthand description. A man-or-woman-for-others. But does this not contradict the very nature of the human person? Are we not each a "being-for-ourselves?" Gifted with intelligence that endows us with power, do we not tend to control the world, making ourselves its center? Is this not our vocation, our history?

Yes; gifted with conscience, intelligence and power each of us is indeed *a* center. But a center called to go out of ourselves, to give ourself to others in love—love, which is our definitive and all-embracing dimension, that which gives meaning to all our other dimensions. Only the one who loves fully realizes himself or herself as a person. To the extent that any of us shuts ourselves off from others we do not become more a person; we becomes less. . . .

Men-and-women-for-others: the paramount objective of Jesuit education—basic, advance, and continuing—must now be to form such men and women. For if there is any substance in our reflections, then this is the prolongation into the modern world of our humanist tradition as derived from the Spiritual Exercises of Saint Ignatius. Only by being a man-or-woman-for-others does one become fully human, not only in the merely natural sense, but in the sense of being the "spiritual" person of Saint Paul. The person filled with the Spirit; and we know whose Spirit that is: the Spirit of Christ, who gave his life for the salvation of the world; the God who, by becoming a human person, became, beyond all others, a Man-for-others, a Woman-for-others.[3]

Love for Christ Poor (From *Final Allocution to the Procurators, Challenge to Religious Life Today, Justice with Faith Today, Recollections and Reflections of Pedro Arrupe, s.j.*)

Nowadays the world does not need words, but lives which cannot be explained except through faith and love for Christ poor.[4]

***

The mystery of poverty springs from the mystery of the *kenosis* of Christ, Christ's emptying of himself. It is a mystery, something that human reason cannot fully comprehend, something we can approach only in the measure that we are enlightened by the Holy Spirit. The problematic of religious poverty is neither sociological nor financial. It is not even merely theological. It is a problematic of faith: of love for Christ poor, poor in the human life he chose for himself, poor in the life of his Mystical Body.

And so, to arrive at a measure of understanding of what poverty means, a double experience is necessary. A faith experience, first of all, of Christ's emptying of himself; but also a lived experience of being really poor. If either of these two experiences is lacking, one cannot really know what religious poverty is. If the mystical experience of Christ's *kenosis* is lacking, one can possibly know what human poverty and misery are, that poverty and misery which we are called upon to fight in themselves and in their effects; but one cannot know what religious poverty is and means. If the personal, lived experience of real poverty is lacking, one may possibly arrive at some knowledge of what the poverty of the historical Christ was and its characteristic traits; but one cannot know what the poverty of poor [people] is in actuality.[5]

***

The poor, the suffering, the disadvantaged, must stand at the very centre of our concern. For they need justice as much as anyone else; only they can neither buy it nor impose it. It was left for God to bring the good news to the poor.

But God is not only the God of the poor. [God] is, in a real sense, God who is poor. For the mystery of the Incarnation has established a special relationship between God and poverty whose meaning goes much deeper than mere compassion. The Scriptures, especially the New Testament, invite us to plumb the depths of that meaning.[6]

***

Nothing is more practical than finding God, that is, than falling in love in a quite absolute, final way. What you are in love with, what seizes your imagination, will affect everything. It will decide what will get you out of bed in the morning, what you will do with your evenings, how you will spend your weekends, what you read, who you know, what breaks your heart, and what amazes you with joy and gratitude. Fall in love, stay in love and it will decide everything.[7]

***

More than ever, I now find myself in the hands of God. This is what I have wanted all my life, from my youth. And this is still the one thing I want. But now there is a difference: the initiative is entirely with God. It is indeed a profound spiritual experience to know and feel myself so totally in His hands.[8]

George Ganss (1905–2000)

The scholarly contributions to the renewal of the Ignatian tradition, begun several decades before the Second Vatican Council by Joseph de Guibert and his colleagues, focused a good deal of attention on the foundational texts of St. Ignatius, above all, his *Spiritual Exercises*. Throughout his own career, de Guibert paid special attention to the dynamic link between the Exercises and the mission of the Society of Jesus.

> We have encountered again that which seems to me to be the most profound influence which the Exercises have exerted on the spirituality of the Society. . . . It seems to me that we cannot avoid being struck by the prominence which all Jesuits give to concern for the service of God. Their orientation is toward service even more than toward union with Him. No matter how highly they esteem this union under all its forms, they are nevertheless ready to sacrifice everything short of that essential union through grace, faith, and charity in order to be able to give a better service to their divine Master.[1]

De Guibert knew that the work he had undertaken for the order was seminal but it is unlikely that he could have envisaged its full import. The Second Vatican Council only a score of years later was to call every Catholic congregation to return to the sources of the graced inspirations of their founders. In that context, de Guibert's patient work triggered a veritable flood of research on the Ignatian sources that in turn offered new ground for research and reflection during subsequent decades. While scholarship and practice have moved beyond his insights in some areas, in one thing, at least, his work remains utterly fresh: he insisted that the whole thrust of the *Spiritual Exercises* and, by extension, the prayerful life of anyone drawn to Ignatian spirituality, be centered on the service of God's kingdom.

In 1960, following the publication of de Guibert's work in French, George Ganss, s.j., a professor of languages at Marquette University, sought permission to translate it into English (along with the *Constitutions* of the Society of Jesus) for his Jesuit colleagues in the United States.[2] From these humble beginnings, Ganss quietly took up the role in the ongoing renewal of the Ignatian tradition pioneered by de Guibert. His dream of a small publishing house dedicated to translating and publishing primary sources of Ignatian spirituality into English became a reality in 1962 when the provincials of the United States appointed him the first director and general editor of the Institute for Jesuit Sources located on the campus of St. Louis University. As its first work the Institute published an English translation of de Guibert's landmark text, *The Jesuits: Their Spiritual Doctrine and Practice.*

The work of translating and publishing primary sources helped drive the renewal of the Society's practice. At the same time, various Jesuit leaders realized the importance of generating and publishing new insights to deepen that renewal. On every continent in the world Jesuits responded to the need to develop contemporary resources that mine the richness of the Society's spiritual and practical history. Similarly, they worked to describe Ignatian spirituality in terms that lay movements and other Ignatian-inspired religious congregations could draw on. Shortly after the conclusion of General Congregation 31 (1965–1966), the U.S. provincials established a seminar to write and publish a series of monographs titled *Studies in the Spirituality of Jesuits.* While generally written by and for Jesuits, most of the monographs have been widely disseminated, read, and discussed by numerous others drawn to the Ignatian charism.

Ganss was the first permanent secretary of the seminar and editor of its various publications, a position he retained along with his work as director of the Institute of Jesuit Sources until he retired in 1986. He continued to translate and work on primary sources until shortly before his death. A bibliography of his work includes translations of primary sources, edited articles, extended introductions, original monographs, and several multivolume projects that witness to his substantial contribution to the renewal of Ignatian spirituality in the English-speaking world. Like St. Alfonsus Rodriguez from another century, George Ganss lived a quiet life of heroic service to the Society during this recent period of intense renewal.

The two excerpts reproduced here reflect Ganss' careful scholarly research into the classic text of Ignatian spirituality, the *Spiritual Exer-*

cises. The first is a scholarly note on the extended title that Ignatius himself gave his work. The second, from an early essay in the *Studies* series, speaks to the way Ignatius intended the text of the *Exercises* to be used.

Eileen Burke-Sullivan and Kevin F. Burke, s.j.

"The End of the Exercises" (From "Endnotes on the *Exercises*" in *The Spiritual Exercises of Saint Ignatius*)

> *Spiritual Exercises*
> *To Overcome Oneself,*
> *And*
> *To Order One's Life,*
> *Without Reaching a Decision*
> *Through Some Disordered Affection*
> *(SpEx 21)*[3]

To "overcome oneself" is the "negative" purpose of the Exercises: a preliminary removal of obstacles, such as sin or disordered inclinations to it. This is usually a first step indispensable to spiritual progress. To this negative end Ignatius immediately adds the genuine, positive, and inspirational aim of the Exercises, eternal salvation. New and enriching aspects of this goal, especially those known from divine revelation, emerge as the exercitant goes through the Exercises, and even subsequently as he or she goes through life in the light of them. In Ignatius' thinking, to "order one's life" is to bring its details into accordance with the Principle and Foundation about to be given in 23.

And yet, what is the essential end of the *Exercises*? Although Ignatius' succinct statement in 21 seems clear at first reading, it has given rise to extensive discussions. With some oversimplification to get to the heart of the matter, the chief writers can be divided into two schools, "electionists" (e.g., L. de Grandmaison) and "perfectionists" (e.g., L. Peeters). De Grandmaison maintained in 1921: The end is to prepare a spiritually minded person to make a wise election of a state of life in which he or she can serve God best. The text as it stands is clearly directed to that end. Peeters objected in 1931: The end and culminating point of the Exercises can only be a union with God which is most intimate and total. An answer unifying both these extremes was written by Joseph de Guibert shortly before his death in 1942 and posthumously published in 1953: Those two ends are complementary, not mutually exclusive. If we consider Ignatius' printed text of 1548 and his process in writing it while winning companions from 1534 onward, the end expressed *in his text* is to facilitate a good election; and that is the supposition which best enables us to interpret the wording of Ignatius' text itself. However, if we consider the uses which he himself made of his text, we see that he gave the exercises to persons whose election was already made (e.g., Xavier and Favre), and that his objective was to lead them to intensive union with God. He found the principles in the text leading to an election to be equally suitable for guiding exercitants to lofty union with God; but he did not trouble himself to state this explicitly by stylistic revisions in the text itself. He left it to directors to adjust the text and its principles flexibly to the personalities and needs of each exercitant.[4]

"Authentic Spiritual Exercises" (From *Studies in the Spirituality of Jesuits*)

In the authentic Exercises, the role of the director was of great importance and original in many respects. . . . An important original feature of Ignatius' book was that it was addressed primarily to the director. It was not a book for a tyro athlete about "How to Play Tennis," but rather one for his coach on "How to Coach a Capable and Eager Player," allowing full play to his own activity, energy, openness to God, and ingenuity under His grace. The role expected of the director can be compared to that of an orchestra leader. On paper is a set of notes. One director or set of musicians can follow them with minute accuracy and still produce a dull performance. Another director can take those same notes, instruments, and musicians, and through them he can create, so that everything is life and inspiration. Ignatius' ideal director had to be like the latter director. His function was to stimulate the exercitant's desires, moderate his progress and speed through the sequence of topics, ask how the contemplations were succeeding, be available for counseling and help in discerning the spirits. But it was also to make himself superfluous, that is, to let God deal directly with the exercitant that he might himself carry on henceforward by energy from within.

After a given contemplation was completed, Ignatius often handed it in written form to the exercitant as an aid for reviewing; but he did not give him the whole sheaf of his notes in advance. After the sheaf became a printed book in 1548, Ignatius was reluctant to communicate it to those who had not first made the Exercises. To Alexis Fontana, who had requested a copy of the book, he wrote on October 8, 1555: "I am sending you a book of the Exercises, that it may be useful to you. . . . The fact is that the force and energy of the Exercises consists in practice and activity, as their very name makes clear; and yet I did not find myself able to refuse your request. However, if possible, the book should be given only after the Exercises have been made." Clearly, therefore, the sheaf of notes, and later the printed book, was the body of the Exercises and the director their life-giving soul.[5]

Josée Gsell (1925–1999) and Christian Life Communities

A s this study has shown, Ignatian spirituality is the heart and foundation of the Society of Jesus. Their spirituality is the first gift that members of the Society give the larger church. But much of Ignatius' experience that grounds the whole way of life happened to him before he and his companions formed the Society, and well before he was ordained a priest. Ignatius was a layperson when he encountered God in his first conversion at Loyola Castle. He was still a layperson when he undertook the months of prayer and penance that resulted in the *Spiritual Exercises*. Many of the first persons with whom he shared the experience were laypeople. Ignatius' way became the inspiration for women's apostolic communities like Mary Ward's institute and thirty-three other women's communities and several orders of men. Further, the Ignatian way from the beginning has shaped the spiritual consciousness of persons who are not called to orders or religious vows, but do experience a call to follow this way of apostolic life.

Shortly before Ignatius died, a young Belgian named John Leunis joined the Society. While in early studies he formed a group for lay students at the Roman College that undertook the Spiritual Exercises. With them he developed a pattern of spirituality that incorporated frequent reception of the sacraments of penance and Eucharist, daily personal prayer, discernment of God's will, reverence for Mary as the prototype of Christian life, and practical work of justice and mercy among neighbors. The members further made lifetime promises to sustain this spiritual life and maintain cordial companionship with other members even after they married and established families. This Marian Congregation of the Roman College became a model for subsequent groups of both youth and adults established by the Jesuits across the world wherever they took up ministry. The terms "Congregation of Mary" and "Sodality of Mary" were used interchangeably to identify the communities that arose from the Roman College model.

Numerous references to the sodalities are found in the writings of the early Jesuits. Antonio Ruiz de Montoya, Matteo Ricci, Roberto de Nobili, Francis Xavier, Pierre Favre, and others described the effectiveness of this instrument for forming men and women committed to service of Christ. While closely associated with the life and work of the Society, these groups never became second or third orders, but remained simply a ministry of the society. There is growing historical research that supports the claim that these groups, and others like them, did much to reform the moral life of Catholics while providing an anchor and mainstay for the Catholic faith in mission lands from Japan to the Americas.[1]

In the late eighteenth century the Society of Jesus was suppressed for nearly forty years in most of the European countries and their colonies but the sodalities were not suppressed. The formation and direction of them, however, was assigned to local bishops. Even after the Jesuits were restored in 1814 the formation of sodality groups was not officially recognized by the church as a Jesuit ministry until the early twentieth century. During that nearly 130-year period many of the sodalities lost their Ignatian character, their mission focus, and their communal grounding.

With papal urging in 1922, the general of the Jesuits, Fr. Ledochowski accepted for the Jesuits the daunting task of working to restore the Ignatian character to the worldwide sodality movement. In 1947 Pope Pius XII confirmed in the apostolic constitution *Bis Saeculari* that all groups attached to the original Roman College sodality were restored to the guidance of the Jesuits. They were to be organized and formed as Ignatian Catholic action groups. By the Second World War, the Jesuits brought about the restoration of lay leadership at all levels of organization.

Vatican II called every ecclesial group to rediscover and renew their original charisms. In line with this, in 1967 the world sodality movement formally adopted *General Principles* (in place of former rules) that deliberately restored the original spirituality and purpose, and changed their name to Christian Life Communities (CLC).[2] In 1971 Pope Paul VI formally suppressed the sodality and recognized Christian Life Communities in its place.

With lay leadership the world community entered a new relationship with the Society of Jesus, a partnership in mission. During General Congregation 35 the Jesuits identified CLC as a community with "roots that are deep in the charism and history of the Society"[3] and expressed an intention of continuing to work together. Father General Adolfo Nicolás, who accepted the role of ecclesial assistant to CLC from Pope Benedict XVI, told the delegates at a world assembly in Portugal in 2008, "We Jesuits are extremely happy to see that the gifts of Ignatius are yours, are spreading and move beyond Jesuit circles and control. . . . It is our joy to see the gifts of Ignatius become our shared patrimony for the good of the Church and the World."[4]

A laywoman from France named Josée Gsell proved to be one of the extraordinary leaders that steered the challenging process of renewal and transformation. Born in 1925 in St. Hippolyte, in the Alsace region of eastern France, Gsell was deeply formed in an apostolic faith through the Christian Agricultural Youth movement[5] during the "Springtime of Catholic Revival"[6] in the years following World War II. In 1960 Gsell moved to Paris seeking theological training from the Jesuits. Deeply imbued with devotion to the Blessed Virgin, and desiring better formation in Ignatian spirituality, she joined the French sodality. In that setting she studied Karl Rahner's theological exposition of the *Spiritual Exercises* and then made the Exercises in a long retreat under Maurice Guiliani, a French Jesuit who pioneered the restoration of individually guided Spiritual Exercises for laypersons according to the Nineteenth Annotation.[7]

In the midst of her long retreat Gsell recognized a call to "help souls," as Ignatius had, by sharing her extraordinary experience and leadership talents with other laypeople. She teamed up with a small group of Jesuits who were guiding members of the French sodalities in the Exercises, and became a national leader in the French federation.

When CLC identified the Spiritual Exercises as the characteristic instrument of member formation, world leaders realized that a strong formation team would have to be established at the world office in Rome. Father Arrupe, the new Jesuit general, recommended Josée Gsell and urged that they hire her as executive secretary with a mandate to develop formation programs grounded in Ignatian spirituality. For sixteen years Gsell traveled to sixty-five nations organizing and leading formation programs for local leaders with strategies for developing small communities of faith, teaching personal and communal discernment of spirits, providing methods for giving the Exercises to persons of every economic strata, and recommending practical ways for first-world members to simplify their lifestyles. All over the world she led institutes on social analysis, and workshops on discovering the greatest needs for service within various settings and social conditions.

In addition to her travels, Gsell kept up a massive correspondence, writing as many as one hundred letters a day when she was in Rome and nearly as many on the road. She participated in the Pontifical Council on the Laity and oversaw CLC's application to the United Nations for recognition as a non-governmental organization (NGO). This gave CLC a permanent presence in the United Nations at both the New York and the Geneva offices. She edited the CLC international journal, *Progressio*, and made certain to highlight key themes of Ignatian spirituality such as the evangelical love for the poor and the companionship of a discerning community. Moreover, she encouraged members to write about these and other Ignatian themes from the perspective of lay members as well as Jesuits, and to do so from all over the world.

Although health concerns forced Gsell to retire from the World Office of CLC in 1987, for another twelve years she offered personal spiritual direction and formation institutes in France. She died at home in Alsace, France, in 1999.

While Gsell's written work was primarily practical correspondence and descriptions of formation programs, she periodically wrote short monographs as supplements for *Progressio*, and short essays in other Ignatian journals. Brief excerpts are included here from an extended meditation on Mary's role in Ignatian spirituality, and from a short life of Fr. Louis Paulussen, S.J., one of her Jesuit partners in the CLC mission. The texts disclose how deeply formed she was in the Ignatian tradition. They also point out the focus and the challenge of lay formation in that tradition.

Eileen Burke-Sullivan

From *Walking the Road with Mary*

The road gradually opened out . . . the road taken by the Savior of the world; the road taken by the Word of God. The road of his humanity; a humanity made possible by love and lived from the soil of poverty and self-donation, the soil uniquely capable of making it fertile. . . .

You saw him take that road, Mary, and you took it with Him. Each of its stages became a stage of your own road, to the point of blending yours completely with his. You were the first to walk after him, first to understand the way of God, first to utter the yes of a saved humanity. . . .

You, Our Lady of all times and all moments, you make it your task to prepare and guide, to alert and strengthen us, so that all will hear the call. You desire that all will advance toward your Son and work for the coming of his Reign. But above all, each person is able to find in you the example of genuine participation in the liberation of humanity to the extent we desire to do so.

Doesn't our desire to be faithful to the CLC way of life bring us, in a privileged way, toward Mary? "We venerate the Mother of God in a special way, and we trust in her intercession to fulfill our vocation. . . ."[8] To go with Mary is to follow the direction of her life: a simple lifestyle lived in solidarity with the poor and oppressed; a life docile to the Spirit, who molds it until it becomes like her Son's. Our service, our availability for others, is the sharing of efforts to become open channels for the gospel message. A plural reality: the CLC members scattered in the various countries of the world each in his or her own mission becomes one, identical vocation shared and binding our community together. Together, we have been called. Together, we must respond. And we entrust the togetherness of our worldwide community to her intercession. . . . "I am the handmaid of the Lord, let what you have said be done to me."[9]

Forming Free Men and Women (From *Father Louis Paulussen, s.j.: Faithful Servant of Grace*)

The General Principles provided us with a written description of the CLC way of life. But how were we to encourage the progress of groups toward real community? There were no easy answers to any of these questions. We felt—and events confirmed this—that not every kind of formation would lead to an experience of the CLC way of life. . . .

The real turning point was 1973, when the first international session on formation was held in Villa Cavalletti, outside Rome, and followed by the Augsburg Assembly. . . 105 members of Christian Life Community, coming from 39 countries, registered for the 15 day session! Clearly, the proposed session was meeting a real need. For the first eight days, all took part in individually guided spiritual Exercises; during the remaining week, they defined and deepened their understanding of the essential aspects of the CLC way of life. Practical teaching, perfectly integrated with the dynamics of the Exercises, would have a lasting effect on the process of growth, a process that must be encouraged within the framework of a serious commitment to CLC. . . .

It would not be enough to provide "a few elements" of spirituality; rather, it was important to give access to it in full and to make clear the demands of the spiritual experience proposed by Ignatius in his Exercises. The purpose was clear: to form free men and women who would be ready to serve others and to promote the concept of "[the dignity of] every person, and the whole person". . . .

Its implementation required, and will always require, formed lay people. . . .

Three years later [with the help of Fr. Paulussen], we were able to prepare for the 1976 Assembly in Manila. The theme for this assembly had been chosen, as usual, in consultation with national communities: "Poor with Christ for a better service."[10]

General Congregations 32 and 34 (1975, 1995)

From its earliest days the Society of Jesus developed a structure of internal governance both inspired by the structures of monastic and mendicant orders yet different from them. For example, the Society did not depend on regularly scheduled meetings of the membership to assign duties and select superiors, but delegated these administrative tasks to the general, the provincials, and in some cases, to local superiors. The Jesuits retained something analogous to the general chapter of the mendicant orders insofar as they invested general congregations with the highest authority in the order. General Congregation 1 met two years after the death of Ignatius to elect his successor as general. Thereafter general congregations were called as circumstances demanded, either to elect a new general or to address serious issues affecting the Society's mission, ministries, and community life.

During the four decades after the Second Vatican Council, which concluded in 1965, the Society of Jesus met in general congregations on four occasions. General Congregation 31 met in two sessions between 1965 and 1966, elected Pedro Arrupe as general, and began to implement the mandates of Vatican II. Father Arrupe called GC 32, which met from December 1974 through March 1975, to address the Society's ongoing effort to renew itself and its mission in the light of the council. In 1983, two years after Fr. Arrupe suffered a debilitating stroke, GC 33 met to elect his successor, Peter Hans Kolvenbach. Father Kolvenbach called GC 34, which met in 1995, to align the Society's law with the Catholic Church's newly revised Code of Canon Law and to reflect on the Society's general direction thirty years after the Second Vatican Council.

Unlike the other chapters in this book which draw on the writings of various individual practitioners of the Ignatian charism, this chapter represents Ignatian spirituality through the "corporate voice" of the Society of Jesus sounding through the documents of General Congregations 32 and 34. The following selections, taken from two of the sixteen decrees of GC 32 and three of the twenty-six decrees of GC 34, shed light on the way the contemporary Society of Jesus embodies the Ignatian charism. These five decrees do not exhaust the richness of the congregations but they accurately capture the emphasis placed by the contemporary Society on the correlation of faith and justice. Selections from the texts have been arranged in five thematic sections. They address, in turn, Jesuit identity today ("What Is It to Be a Jesuit?"), the Society's commitment to faith and justice ("Our Mission Today"), the enormous challenge of evangelization in a world riven by poverty and injustice ("A New Challenge"), a statement of the Society's commitment to promote the equality of women and men and combat sexism within its own body and in the world ("Jesuits and the Situation of Women"), and a brief note on the Ignatian *magis* ("The *Magis*").

Kevin F. Burke, s.j.

What Is It to Be a Jesuit? (From GC 32, Decree 2 and GC 34, Decree 26)

What is it to be a Jesuit? It is to know that one is a sinner, yet called to be a companion of Jesus as Ignatius was: Ignatius, who begged the Blessed Virgin to "place him with her Son," and who then saw the Father himself ask Jesus, carrying his Cross, to take this pilgrim into his company.

What is it to be a companion of Jesus today? It is to engage, under the standard of the Cross, in the crucial struggle of our time: the struggle for faith and that struggle for justice which it includes. (From GC 32.2, 1–2)

***

In remorse, gratitude, and astonishment—but above all with passionate love—first Ignatius, and then every Jesuit after him, has turned prayerfully to "Christ our Lord hanging on the Cross before me" and has asked of himself, "What have I done for Christ? What am I doing for Christ? What must I do for Christ?" The questions well up from a heart moved with profound gratitude and love. This is the foundational grace that binds Jesuits to Jesus and to one another. "What is it to be a Jesuit today? It is to know that one is a sinner yet called to be a companion of Jesus as Ignatius was" [GC 32]. The mission of the reconciled sinner is the mission of reconciliation: the work of faith doing justice. A Jesuit freely gives what he has freely received: the gift of Christ's redeeming love. (From GC 34.26, 4–5)

Our Mission Today (From GC 32, Decrees 2 and 4, and GC 34, Decree 2)

The mission of the Society of Jesus today is the service of faith of which the promotion of justice is an absolute requirement. For reconciliation with God demands the reconciliation of people with one another.

In one form or another, this has always been the mission of the Society; but it gains new meaning and urgency in the light of the needs and aspirations of the men and women of our time, and it is in that light that we examine it anew. We are confronted today, in fact, by a whole series of new challenges. (From GC 32.4, 2–3)

***

The Church, whose mission we share, exists not for itself but for humanity, bearing the proclamation of God's love and casting light on the inner gift of that love. Its aim is the realization of the Kingdom of God in the whole of human society, not only in the life to come but also in this life. We exercise our Jesuit mission within the total evangelizing mission of the Church. This mission is "a single but complex reality which develops in a variety of ways": through the integral dimensions of life witness, proclamation, conversion, inculturation, the genesis of local churches, dialogue and the promotion of the justice willed by God [John Paul II]. Within this framework, in accordance with our charism, our tradition, and the approval and encouragement of popes through the years, the contemporary Jesuit mission is the service of faith and the promotion in society of "that justice of the Gospel which is the embodiment of God's love and saving mercy" [GC 33]. . . .

The mission of the Society derives from our continuing experience of the Crucified and Risen Christ who invites us to join him in preparing the world to become the completed Kingdom of God. The focus of Christ's mission is the prophetic proclamation of the Gospel that challenges people in the name of the Kingdom of his Father; we are to preach that Kingdom in poverty. He calls us to be at the very heart of the world's experience as it receives this promise of the Kingdom and is brought to receive God's gift in its fullness. It is still an experience of the Cross, in all its anguish and with all its power, because the enigmas of sin and death are still part of the reality of the world. He calls us "to help men and women disengage themselves from the tarnished and confused image that they have of themselves in order to discover that they are, in God's light, completely like Christ" [GC 32]. And so we undertake all our ministries with a confidence that the Lord takes us, as he did Ignatius, as his servants—not because we are strong, but because he says to us, as he said to St. Paul, "My grace is sufficient for you, for my power is made perfect in weakness" (2 Cor. 12:9). (From GC 34.2, 3, 6)

***

Two-thirds of humankind have not yet had God's salvation in Jesus Christ proclaimed to them in a manner that wins belief, while in societies anciently Christian a dominant secularism is closing [people's] minds and hearts to the divine dimensions of all reality, blinding them to the fact that while all things on the face of the earth are, indeed, created for [the sake of humans], it is only that [they] might attain to the end for which [they themselves were] created: the praise, reverence, and service of God.

Ignorance of the Gospel on the part of some, and rejection of it by others are intimately related to the many grave injustices prevalent in the world today. Yet it is in the light of the Gospel that [people] will most clearly see that injustice springs from sin, personal and collective, and that it is made all the more oppressive by being built into economic, social, political, and cultural institutions of world-wide scope and overwhelming power.

Conversely, the prevalence of injustice in a world where the very survival of the human race depends on [people] caring for and sharing with one another is one of the principal obstacles to belief: belief in a God who is justice because he is love.

Thus, the way to faith and the way to justice are inseparable ways. It is up this undivided road, this steep road, that the pilgrim Church must travel and toil. Faith and justice are undivided in the Gospel which teaches that "faith makes its power felt through love" [Gal. 5.6]. They cannot therefore be divided in our purpose, our action, our life.

Moreover, the service of faith and the promotion of justice cannot be for us simply one ministry among others. It must be the integrating factor of all our ministries; and not only of our ministries but of our inner life as individuals, as communities, and as a world-wide brotherhood. This is what our Congregation means by a decisive choice. It is the choice that underlies and determines all the other choices embodied in its declarations and directives. (From GC 32.2, 5–9)

***

We are witnesses of a Gospel which links the love of God to the service of [people], and that inseparably. In a world where the power of economic, social and political structures is now appreciated and the mechanisms and laws governing them are now understood, service according to the Gospel cannot dispense with a carefully planned effort to exert influence on those structures.

We must bear in mind, however, that our efforts to promote justice and human freedom on the social and structural level, necessary though they are, are not sufficient of themselves. Injustice must be attacked at its roots which are in the human heart by transforming those attitudes and habits which beget injustice and foster the structures of oppression. (From GC 32.4, 31–32)

***

Ours is a service of faith and of the radical implications of faith in a world where it is becoming easier to settle for something less than faith and less than justice. We recognize, along with many of our contemporaries, that without faith, without the eye of love, the human world seems too evil for God to be good, for a good God to exist. But faith recognizes that God is acting, through Christ's love and the power of the Holy Spirit, to destroy the structures of sin which afflict the bodies and hearts of his children. Our Jesuit mission touches something fundamental in the human heart: the desire to find God in a world scarred by sin, and then to live by his Gospel in all its implications. This, the instinct to live fully in God's love and thereby to promote a shared, lasting human good, is what we address by our vocation to serve faith and promote justice of God's Kingdom. Jesus Christ invites us, and through us the people we serve, to move, in conversion of heart, "from solidarity with sin to solidarity with him for humanity," and to promote the Kingdom in all its aspects [P. Kolvenbach]. (From GC 34.2, 11)

A New Challenge (From GC 32, Decree 4)

There is a new challenge to our apostolic mission in a fact without precedent in the history of [humankind]: today, more than two billion human beings have no knowledge of God the Father and His Son, Jesus Christ, whom He has sent, yet feel an increasing hunger for the God they already adore in the depths of their hearts without knowing Him explicitly.

There is a new challenge to our apostolic mission in that many of our contemporaries, dazzled and even dominated by the achievements of the human mind, forgetting or rejecting the mystery of [the human being's] ultimate meaning, have thus lost the sense of God.

There is a new challenge to our apostolic mission in a world increasingly interdependent but, for all that, divided by injustice: injustice not only personal but institutionalized: built into economic, social, and political structures that dominate the life of nations and the international community. . . .

There are millions of men and women in our world, specific people with names and faces, who are suffering from poverty and hunger, from the unjust distribution of wealth and resources and from the consequences of racial, social, and political discrimination. Not only the quality of life but human life itself is under constant threat. It is becoming more and more clear that despite the opportunities offered by an ever more serviceable technology, we are simply not willing to pay the price of a more just and more humane society.

At the same time, people today are somehow aware that their problems are not just social and technological, but personal and spiritual. They have a feeling that what is at stake here is the very meaning of humanity: [our] future and [our] destiny. People are hungry: hungry not just for bread, but for the Word of God. (Deut. 8.3; Mt. 4.4). For this reason the Gospel should be preached with a fresh vigor, for it is in a position once again to make itself heard. At first sight God seems to have no place in public life, nor even in private awareness. Yet everywhere, if we only know how to look, we can see that people are groping towards an experience of Christ and waiting in hope for His Kingdom of love, of justice and of peace. (From GC 32.4, 20–21)

Jesuits and the Situation of Women (From GC 34, Decree 14)

General Congregation 33 made a brief mention of the "unjust treatment and exploitation of women." It was part of a list of injustices in a context of new needs and situations which Jesuits were called to address in the implementation of our mission. We wish to consider this question more specifically and substantially on this occasion. This is principally because, assisted by the general rise in consciousness concerning this issue, we are more aware than previously that it is indeed a central concern of any contemporary mission which seeks to integrate faith and justice. It has a universal dimension in that it involves men and women everywhere. To an increasing extent it cuts across barriers of class and culture. It is of personal concern to those who work with us in our mission, especially lay and religious women.

The dominance of men in their relationship with women has found expression in many ways. It has included discrimination against women in educational opportunities, the disproportionate burden they are called upon to bear in family life, paying them a lesser wage for the same work, limiting their access to positions of influence when admitted to public life, and, sadly but only too frequently, outright violence against women themselves. . . .

The legacy of systematic discrimination against women is embedded within the economic, social, political, religious, and even linguistic structures of our societies. It is often part of an even deeper cultural prejudice and stereotype. Many women, indeed, feel that men have been slow to recognize the full humanity of women. They often experience a defensive reaction from men when they draw attention to this blindness. . . .

Church social teaching, especially within the last ten years, has reacted strongly against this continuing discrimination and prejudice. . . .

The tone of this ecclesial reflection on Scripture makes it clear that there is an urgency in the challenge to translate theory into practice not only outside but also within the Church itself.

The Society of Jesus accepts this challenge and our responsibility for doing what we can as men and as a male religious order. We do not pretend or claim to speak for women. However, we do speak out of what we have learned from women about ourselves and our relationship with them. . . .

We are conscious of the damage to the People of God brought about in some cultures by the alienation of women who no longer feel at home in the Church and who are not able with integrity to transmit Catholic values to their families, friends, and colleagues.

In response, we Jesuits first ask God for the grace of conversion. We have been part of a civil and ecclesial tradition that has offended against women. And, like many men, we have a tendency to convince ourselves that there is no problem. However unwittingly, we have often contributed to a form of clericalism which has reinforced male domination with an ostensibly divine sanction. By making this declaration we wish to react personally and collectively, and do what we can to change this regrettable situation. . . .

We wish to specify more concretely at least some ways in which Jesuits may better respond to this challenge to our lives and mission. . . .

In the first place, we invite all Jesuits to listen carefully and courageously to the experience of women. Many women feel that men simply do not listen to them. There is no substitute for such listening. More than anything else it will bring about change. Unless we listen, any action we may take in this area, no matter how well intentioned, is likely to bypass the real concerns of women and to confirm male condescension and reinforce male dominance. Listening, in a spirit of partnership and equality, is the most practical response we can make and is the foundation for our mutual partnership to reform unjust structures.

Second, we invite all Jesuits, as individuals and through their institutions, to align themselves in solidarity with women. . . .

Above all we want to commit the Society in a more formal and explicit way to regard this solidarity with women as integral to our mission. In this way we hope that the whole Society will regard this work for reconciliation between women and men in all its forms as integral to its interpretation of ["Our Mission Today" (GC 32)] for our times. We know that a reflective and sustained commitment to bring about this respectful reconciliation can flow only from our God of love and justice, who reconciles all and promises a world in which "there is neither Jew nor Greek, there is neither slave nor free, there is neither male nor female, for you are all one in Christ Jesus" (Gal. 3:28). (From GC 34.14, 1–3, 5, 6, 7, 8–9, 11, 12, 13, 16)

The *Magis* (From GC 34, Decree 26)

The *magis* is not simply one among others in a list of Jesuit characteristics. It permeates them all. The entire life of Ignatius was a pilgrim search for the *magis*, the ever greater glory of God, the ever fuller service of our neighbor, the more universal good, the more effective apostolic means. . . .

Jesuits are never content with the *status quo*, the known, the tried, the already existing. We are constantly driven to discover, redefine, and reach out for the *magis*. For us, frontiers and boundaries are not obstacles or ends, but new challenges to be faced, new opportunities to be welcomed. Indeed, ours is a holy boldness, "a certain apostolic aggressivity," typical of our way of proceeding. (From GC 34.26, 26–27)

Afterword

This book emerged from our efforts to comb the nearly five-hundred-year-old Ignatian tradition for a variety of voices to represent that tradition to the twenty-first century. Interestingly, during the time that we were finishing the book, the Society of Jesus convened its thirty-fifth general congregation. This historic meeting accepted the resignation of the Society's twenty-ninth general, Fr. Peter Hans Kolvenbach, s.j., and elected his successor, Fr. Adolfo Nicolás, s.j. Before concluding on March 6, 2008, the congregation also published a modest collection of six decrees.

Many of the delegates to General Congregation 35 testified that the congregation spoke its most important "word" through its choice of the new superior general. "The feeling continues that in electing Adolfo Nicolás," one delegate wrote to friends back home, "we have not just chosen a good leader, but we have also said perhaps the most important thing we can say as a Congregation about where the Society should go and how we should proceed. In a sense, his election will be the chief 'decree' of the Society gathered together in this congregation."[1] The congregation clearly ratified the direction taken by the Society in recent congregations, most notably GC 32 and GC 34. Yet its own words provide a glimpse into the future of the Ignatian tradition both as that tradition is embodied in the Society of Jesus itself and as it lives beyond the Society in the many religious and lay bodies, the many partners in mission who consciously adopt as their own charism the spirit of St. Ignatius.

We conclude this volume with two brief selections. The first, "To All the Nations," comes from the homily given by Fr. Adolfo Nicolás the day after the Congregation elected him new superior general of the Society of Jesus. Characteristically, his focus is on the Christian mission to which the Society is committed, a mission that reaches to the ends of the earth and today touches new and often invisible "nations, other non-geographic communities, human communities, that claim our aid."

The second decree of GC 35, *A Fire that Kindles Other Fires: Rediscovering Our Charism*, provides our final selection. This moving text affirms the truth that every tradition must continually renew itself, indeed must reinvent itself, in order to remain faithful to its core inspiration. This involves discerning the needs and hungers of the world to which we are sent and discovering anew the frontiers to which God sends us on mission. These words, written specifically to the members of the Society of Jesus, speak for all of us who find ourselves within the Ignatian tradition.

Kevin F. Burke, S.J.

To All the Nations (From "Homily of Fr. Adolfo Nicolás")

> *I will make you a light to the nations,*
> *that my salvation may reach to the ends of the earth. (Is 49:6)*

All represented nations are gathered here today. All, everyone, is represented here. However, nations continue to open up. I ask myself today, which are those "nations"? Indeed, all geographic nations are here today. However, there may be other nations, other non-geographic communities, human communities, that claim our aid: the poor, the marginalized, the excluded. In this globalized world of ours the number of those excluded by all is increasing. Those excluded are diminished, since our society only has room for the big and not the small. All those who are disadvantaged, manipulated, all of these may perhaps be for us those "nations"—the nations that need the prophetic message of God.

Yesterday after the election, after the first shock, there came the moment of fraternal aid. All of you greeted me very affectionately, offering your support and help. One of you whispered to me: "Don't forget the poor!" Perhaps this is the most important greeting of all, just as Paul turns to the wealthier churches of his time requesting aid for the poor of Jerusalem. Don't forget the poor: these are our "nations." These are the nations for whom salvation is still a dream, a wish. Perhaps it may be in their midst, but they don't realize it.

And the others? The others are our collaborators, if they share our same perspective, if they have the same heart Christ has given us. And if they have a bigger heart and an even greater vision, then we are their collaborators. What counts is health, salvation, the joy of the poor. What counts, what is real, is hope, salvation, health. And we want that this salvation, this health, be an explosion of salvation that reaches out everywhere. This is what the prophet Isaiah is talking about: That salvation may reach and touch everyone. A salvation according to God's heart, will, Spirit.[2]

From *A Fire that Kindles Other Fires* (GC 35, Decree 2)

The Society of Jesus has carried a flame for nearly five hundred years through innumerable social and cultural circumstances that have challenged it intensely to keep that flame alive and burning. Things are no different today. In a world that overwhelms people with a multiplicity of sensations, ideas, and images, the Society seeks to keep the fire of its original inspiration alive in a way that offers warmth and light to our contemporaries. It does this by telling a story that has stood the test of time, despite the imperfections of its members and even of the whole body, because of the continued goodness of God, who has never allowed the fire to die. Our attempt here is to present it anew as a living narrative that, when brought into contact with the life-stories of people today, can give them meaning and provide focus in a fragmented world. . . .

To find divine life at the depths of reality is a mission of hope given to us Jesuits. We travel again the path taken by Ignatius. As in his experience so too in ours, because a space of interiority is opened where God works in us, we are able to see the world as a place in which God is at work and which is full of his appeals and of his presence. Thus we enter, with Christ who offers living water, into the dry and lifeless areas of the world. Our mode of proceeding is to trace the footprints of God *everywhere*, knowing that the Spirit of Christ is at work in all places and situations and in all activities and mediations that seek to make him more present in the world. This mission of attempting "to feel and to taste" (*sentir y gustar*) the presence and activity of God in all the persons and circumstances of the world places us Jesuits at the centre of a tension pulling us both to God and to the world at the same time. Thus arises, for Jesuits on mission, a set of polarities, Ignatian in character, that accompanies our being firmly rooted in God at all times, while simultaneously being plunged into the heart of the world.

Being and doing; contemplation and action; prayer and prophetic living; being completely united with Christ and completely inserted in the world with him as an apostolic body: all of these polarities mark deeply the life of a Jesuit and express both its essence and its possibilities. The Gospels show Jesus in deep, loving relationship with his Father and, at the same time, completely given over to his mission among men and women. He is perpetually in motion: from God, for others. This is the Jesuit pattern too: with Christ on mission, ever contemplative, ever active. It is the grace—also the creative challenge—of our apostolic religious life that it must live this tension between prayer and action, between mysticism and service. . . .

Serving Christ's mission today means paying special attention to its *global* context. This context requires us to act as a universal body with a universal mission, realising at the same time the radical diversity of our situations. It is as a worldwide community—and, simultaneously, as a network of local communities—that we seek to serve others across the world. Our mission of faith and justice, dialogue of religions and cultures has acquired dimensions that no longer allow us to conceive of the world as composed of separate entities; we must see it as a unified whole in which we depend upon one another. Globalization, technology, and environmental concerns have challenged our traditional boundaries and have enhanced our awareness that we bear a common responsibility for the welfare of the entire world and its development in a sustainable and life-giving way.

Today's consumerist cultures do not foster passion and zeal but rather addiction and compulsion. They demand resistance. A compassionate response to these cultural malaises will be necessary and unavoidable if we are to share in the lives of our contemporaries. In such changing circumstances, our responsibility as Jesuits to collaborate at multiple levels has become an imperative. Thus our provinces must work ever more together. So also must we work with others: religious men and women of other communities; lay persons; members of ecclesial movements; people who share our values but not our beliefs; in short, all persons of good will.

God has created a world with diverse inhabitants, and this is good. Creation expresses the rich beauty of this lovable world: people working, laughing, and thriving together are signs that God is alive among us. However, diversity becomes problematic when the differences between people are lived in such a way that some prosper at the expense of others who are excluded in such a way that people fight, killing each other, and are intent on destruction.

Then God in Christ suffers in and with the world, which he wants to renew. Precisely here is our mission situated. It is here that we must discern our mission according to the criteria of the *magis* and the more universal good. God is present in the darkness of life intent on making all things new. God needs collaborators in this endeavour: people whose grace consists in being received under the banner of his Son. "Nations" beyond geographical definitions await us, "nations" that today include those who are poor and displaced, those who are profoundly lonely, those who ignore God's existence and those who use God as an instrument for political purposes. There are new "nations," and we have been sent to them. (From GC 35.2.1, 8–9, 20–22)

Notes

Introduction

1. Pope Benedict, XVI, "Address of His Holiness Benedict the Sixteenth to the 35th General Congregation of the Society of Jesus" (February 21, 2008). Creighton University Online Ministries, http://www.creighton.edu/CollaborativeMinistry/GC35/CG35_21_02_2008_attachment_eng.doc.

2. This number is not arbitrary, but is drawn from a short report by Sr. Jeanne-Françoise de Jaegger, Congregation La Retraite, published in an international compendium of articles, reports, and bibliographies, "Ignatian Spirituality Since GC32," by the Ignatian Spirituality Center (CIS), Rome 20 (1978): 89–93.

3. The third degree of humility represents the apex of the graced desire to serve the reign of God. It is given to those who, for love of Jesus, follow him in the most difficult and dangerous of missions.

The Ignatian Tradition

1. The story is fictitious, but it attempts to capture a sense of what actually might have been, based on the witnessed accounts or historical data of Ignatius' life and the process he went through to tell his story for the sake of his Jesuit followers. This method of imagining a scene—even to imagining the physical setting or the weather, smelling the flowers blooming, hearing the voices speaking, etc.—is called "composition of place." It is one of a number of methods of prayer that Ignatius taught. Those who practice Ignatian spirituality will, for example, frequently undertake compositions of place to imagine the context of Jesus' sayings and deeds as he lived his human life.

2. Ignatius of Loyola, *Autobiography, in Ignatius of Loyola: Spiritual Exercises and Selected Works*, ed. and trans. George E. Ganss et al., Classics of Western Spirituality Series (New York: Paulist, 1991), 18.

3. Baldassare Castiglione describes the kind of person Ignatius was expected to become by his appointment to the court of de Cueller. "So in jousts and tournaments, in riding, and handling every kind of weapon, as well as in the festivities, games and musical performances, in short, in all the activities appropriate to a well-born gentleman, everyone at his court strove to behave in such a way as to be judged worthy of the Duke's noble company" (Baldassare Castiglione, *The Book of the Courtier*, trans. George Bull [London: Penguin Books, 1967], 42).

4. *Autobiography*, 68.

5. Ibid., 71.

6. *The Spiritual Exercises of Saint Ignatius: A Translation and Commentary,* ed. and trans. George E. Ganss (St. Louis, MO: Institute of Jesuit Sources, 1992). Throughout this book citations to the text of the *Spiritual Exercises* will be identified in the classical method that employs paragraph numbers, i.e., SpEx 54. One can thus find the reference in any translation or version of the book. Such citations will be located within the text rather than in endnotes. It should be noted that throughout this book we distinguish the written text of the *Spiritual Exercises* from the act of doing the Spiritual Exercises (or directing another who is doing them) by placing the former in italics.

7. Various commentators and historians of the Spiritual Exercises have pointed out that Ignatius delayed leading Pierre Favre through the process until it was clear that he had received the foundational grace of experiencing God's a priori love. Ignatius knew from his own experience that Favre's religious scruples could be traced to a lack of this sensible experience. John W. O'Malley, s.j., points out that the commitment of the first companions to this foundational principle opened them to accusations of attempting to earn God's favor, although "their best and more fundamental statements insisted on the primacy of grace and the necessity of utter commitment of oneself to its movements" (John W. O'Malley, "Some Distinctive Characteristics of Jesuit Spirituality in the Sixteenth Century," in *Jesuit Spirituality: A Now and Future Resource,* eds. John W. O'Malley, John W. Padberg, and Vincent T. O'Keefe (Chicago, IL: Loyola University Press, 1990), 17.

8. The citations in this paragraph are from Louis Puhl's translation of the *Spiritual Exercises*; see Ignatius of Loyola, *Spiritual Exercises of Saint Ignatius,* trans. Louis J. Puhl (Chicago, IL: Loyola Press, 1968).

Ignatius of Loyola (1491–1556)

1. *A Pilgrim's Journey: The Autobiography of Ignatius of Loyola,* trans. Joseph N. Tylenda (Wilmington, DE: Michael Glazier, 1985), 12–15.

2. Ibid., 35–39.

3. Ibid., 109–13.

4. *The Constitutions of the Society of Jesus,* trans. George E. Ganss (St. Louis, MO: The Institute of Jesuit Sources, 1970), 309–11.

Mary Ward (1585–1645)

1. *Till God Will: Mary Ward Through Her Writings,* ed. M. Emmanuel Orchard (London: Darton, Longman and Todd, 1985), 53.

2. Orchard's edition of Ward's writings uses the literal English cognate "verity" (from the Latin *veritas*), which is little used in contemporary English. The term literally means truth, thus we have elected to emend her text with the word "truth" each time "verity" is stated.

3. The actual English phrase that Ward uses is "preventing grace." The root of the term "preventing" is the Latin verb *praeveniens* (to come before; to precede); it is sometimes rendered with the strict English cognate, "prevenient." Ward uses the term "preventing" to mean preceding, not the usual current meaning of "preventing," i.e., keeping something from happening. Given the potential for misunderstanding "preventing" and the obscurity of the term "prevenient," we have twice elected to emend her text by using the term "preceding."

4. *Till God Will,* 64–65.

5. Ibid., 56–58.

6. Mary is quoting St. Richard Gwyn (one of the English martyrs) who stated on the scaffold at Wrexham, 1584, "Weep not for me, for I do but pay the rent before the rent-day."

7. *Till God Will*, 51, 52–53, 105–9.

Jerome Nadal (1507–1580)

1. John W. O'Malley, *The First Jesuits* (Cambridge, MA: Harvard University Press, 1993), 64.

2. Many of Nadal's writings are not yet published in English, although the Institute of Jesuit Sources is working to remedy that lacuna.

3. *Instructions on Prayer*, unpublished manuscript from MHSI, trans. Martin O'Keefe, vol. 4 (St. Louis, MO: The Institute of Jesuit Sources), 576–78, 672–81.

4. Joseph Conwell, *Walking in the Spirit* (St. Louis, MO: The Institute of Jesuit Sources, 2003), xxi–xxii.

5. Thomas Clancy, *The Conversational Word of God* (St. Louis, MO: The Institute of Jesuit Sources, 1978), 52–54.

6. Joseph DeGuibert, *The Jesuits: Their Spiritual Doctrine and Practice*, ed. George Ganss, trans. William Young (St. Louis, MO: The Institute of Jesuit Sources, 1964), 204–5.

Pierre Favre (1506–1546)

1. *The Spiritual Writings of Pierre Favre: The* Memoriale *and Selected Letters and Instructions*, ed. and trans. Edmund Murphy and Martin Palmer (St. Louis, MO: The Institute of Jesuit Sources, 1996), 32. In note 70 in their text, Murphy and Padberg indicate that this is taken from a letter that Rodrigues wrote two years before his own death in 1579. The letter is in volume 24 of the *Monumenta Historica Societatis Iesu (MHSI)*, the multivolume collection of over one hundred volumes published in Madrid in the early twentieth century.

2. A *memoriale* or spiritual diary is a form of literature as old as Saint Paul in the Christian tradition. It was a literary form that was made especially popular in the late Middle Ages under the influence of the lay movement known as the *Devotio Moderna*. One of the better-known examples of this form of Christian humanism, the *Imitation of Christ* by Thomas à Kempis, deeply influenced Ignatius and was admired by the Renaissance scholar, Erasmus.

3. *The Spiritual Writings of Pierre Favre*, 279–80, 292–93, 307–8, 309.

4. Ibid., 321–23, 373–75, 379–81, and 383–85.

Francis Xavier (1506–1552)

1. Xavier is quoting the first and second annotations or instructions of *The Spiritual Exercises* in this passage [eds.].

2. Francis Xavier, *The Letters and Instructions of Francis Xavier*, trans. M. Joseph Costelloe (St. Louis, MO: The Institute of Jesuit Sources, 1992), 67–68, 141–42, 344–45, 348.

Roberto de Nobili (1577–1656)

1. *Preaching Wisdom to the Wise: Three Treatises by Roberto de Nobili, s.j., Missionary and Scholar in 17ᵗʰ-Century India*, trans. and ed. Anand Amaladass and Francis X. Clooney (St. Louis, MO: The Institute of Jesuit Sources, 2000), 53, 195.

2. Ibid., 265–70.

Antonio Ruiz de Montoya (1585–1652)

1. Elizabeth Jones, *Gentlemen and Jesuits: Quests for Glory and Adventure in the Early Days of New France* (Toronto: University of Toronto Press, 1986). The most enduring French settlement in the new world north of Florida is Port Royal, Nova Scotia, established some years before the city of Quebec. Two Jesuits, Pierre Biard and Enemond Massé, were among the early settlers and served as missionaries to the native peoples in the Maritime Provinces.

2. The word comes from the Spanish verb *reducir*, which in the sixteenth century meant to gather into small communities. The English word in this context has the specialized meaning of small community and does not mean "that which has been reduced." See C. J. McNaspy, *Lost Cities of Paraguay: Art and Architecture of the Jesuit Reductions, 1607–1767* (Chicago, IL: Loyola University Press, 1982) for an extended contemporary discussion of this missionary project of the Jesuits.

3. These same stories served as the basis for Robert Bolt's screenplay of the award-winning film *The Mission*, VHS, directed by Roland Joffé (Enigma Productions: 1986).

4. Antonio Ruiz de Montoya, *The Spiritual Conquest*, trans. John P. Leonard and Martin E. Palmer (St. Louis, MO: The Institute of Jesuit Sources, 1993), 100–101, 105–6, 109.

5. Ibid., 129–33, 134.

Citizenship and Prophecy

1. Ignacio Ellacuría and Jon Sobrino, eds., *Mysterium Liberationis: Fundamental Concepts of Liberation Theology* (Maryknoll, NY: Orbis Books, 1994), 273.

Edmund Campion (1540–1581)

1. "Campion's Brag" from Catholic Information Network, http://www.cin.org/saints/campion-brag.html.

Alfred Delp (1907–1945)

1. From *Alfred Delp, s.j.: Prison Writings*, intro. by Thomas Merton (Maryknoll, NY: Orbis Books, 2004), 10–11.

2. From ibid., 16–17.

3. From ibid., 155, 158–62.

4. From ibid., 162–63.

Ignacio Ellacuría (1930–1989)

1. From Ignacio Ellacuría, *Escritos Teológicos*, trans. Kevin F. Burke, vol. 2 (San Salvador: UCA Editores, 2000–2002), 602.

2. From ibid., 86.

3. From ibid., 134.

4. From Ignacio Ellacuría and Jon Sobrino, eds., *Mysterium Liberationis: Fundamental Concepts of Liberation Theory* (Maryknoll, NY: Orbis Books, 1994), 590.

5. From ibid., 289–90.

6. From *Escritos Teológicos*, trans. Kevin F. Burke, vol. 1 (San Salvador: UCA Editores, 2000–2002), 148.

7. From Ignacio Ellacuría, *Freedom Made Flesh: The Mission of Christ and His Church*, trans. John Drury (Maryknoll, NY: Orbis Books, 1976), 134–35.

8. From Ellacuría and Sobrino, *Mysterium Liberationis*, 544.

9. From ibid., 272, 273.

10. From ibid., 543.

Pierre Teilhard de Chardin (1881–1955)

1. From Pierre Teilhard de Chardin, *The Divine Milieu: An Essay on the Interior Life* (New York: Harper and Brothers Publishers, 1960), 89.

2. From ibid., 90.

3. From ibid., 98.

4. From Pierre Teilhard de Chardin, *The Phenomenon of Man*, trans. Bernard Wall (New York: Harper and Row, 1959), 266.

5. From ibid., 283.

6. From Teilhard de Chardin, *The Divine Milieu*, 114–15.

7. From Pierre Teilhard de Chardin, *Toward the Future*, trans. René Hague (New York: Harcourt Brace Jovanovich, 1975), 87.

8. From Pierre Teilhard de Chardin, *Hymn of the Universe*, trans. Simon Bartholomew (New York: Harper and Row, 1965), 23.

9. From Pierre Teilhard de Chardin, *The Making of a Mind: Letters from a Soldier-Priest*, 1914–1919, trans. René Hague (New York: Harper and Row, 1965), 57.

Bernard Lonergan (1904–1984)

1. Bernard Lonergan, *Method in Theology* (Toronto: University of Toronto Press, 1971, 1990), xi.

2. From Bernard Lonergan, *Insight: A Study of Human Understanding* (Toronto: University of Toronto Press, 1957; Fifth Edition Revised and Augmented, 1992), 494–97, 499, 501–2.

3. From Bernard Lonergan, *A Second Collection: Papers*, eds. William F. J. Ryan and Bernard J. Tyrrell (Philadelphia, PA: Westminster Press, 1974; and Toronto: University of Toronto Press, 1993), 55–58.

Karl Rahner (1904–1984)

1. Although this piece was later published in Rahner's *Schriften zur Theologie*, an English translation was not included in the companion volume of *Theological Investigations*. The selections here were translated by J. Matthew Ashley; this translation has not been previously published.

2. In the introduction to this essay Rahner's "Ignatius" makes it clear that he is speaking from the perspective of eternity, not from that of his time on earth (the sixteenth century). More important, he is speaking to us today in our own time. Thus, when "Ignatius" speaks here from "my perspective" he means the perspective of eternity and the beatific vision. This is important for correctly interpreting Rahner's mystical theology. Rahner was concerned about how to distinguish between the immediacy of mystical experience during this life and the immediacy that is only possible in and through the beatific vision [eds.].

3. The German is *dressieren*, which means to train (an animal) or break in (a horse) [trans.].

Daniel Seghers (1590–1661)

1. We are indebted to Prof. Mia M. Mochizuki, PhD, for her assistance on the biographical material and the interpretation of Daniel Seghers' masterpiece, *Madonna and Child with Garlands.*

Gerard Manley Hopkins (1844–1889)

1. We are indebted to Prof. Francis X. McAloon, s.j., for his assistance on the biographical material on Hopkins and the interpretation of Hopkins' poetry in the light of the Ignatian tradition.

2. *The Poems of Gerard Manley Hopkins,* ed. W. H. Gardner and N. H. MacKenzie, 4th ed. (London: Oxford University Press, 1967).

William Lynch (1908–1987)

1. We are indebted to Prof. John Kane, PhD, whose recently completed manuscript, *Passion, Polarization, and Imagination: William F. Lynch, s.j., and a Spirituality of Public Life,* provides the biographical background and much of the interpretative depth behind this chapter.

2. William F. Lynch, s.j., "Me and the East River," *New York Images* 1 (Spring 1984): 5.

3. From William F. Lynch, *Images of Faith: An Exploration of the Ironic Imagination* (Notre Dame, IN: University of Notre Dame Press, 1973), 80–82.

4. From William F. Lynch, *Images of Hope: Imagination as Healer of the Hopeless* (Baltimore, MD: Helicon Press, 1965), 35.

5. From William F. Lynch, *Christ and Prometheus: A New Image of the Secular* (Notre Dame, IN: University of Notre Dame Press, 1970), 23, 25.

6. From Lynch, *Images of Hope,* 26–27, 31–32, 105–7, 116–17.

7. From William F. Lynch, *Christ and Apollo: The Dimensions of the Literary Imagination* (New York: Sheed and Ward, 1960), 64–67.

Pedro Arrupe (1907–1991)

1. Pedro Arrupe, "Hiroshima," in *A Planet to Heal: Reflections and Forecasts* (Rome: Ignatian Center of Spirituality, 1975), 30.

2. Pedro Arrupe, "The Trinitarian Inspiration of the Ignatian Charism," in *The Spiritual Legacy of Pedro Arrupe, s.j.* (Rome: Jesuit Curia, 1985), 105–6.

3. Pedro Arrupe, "Men for Others," address by Pedro Arrupe presented to the Tenth International Congress of Jesuit Alumni of Europe, Valencia, Spain, July 31, 1973 (Washington, DC: Jesuit Secondary Education Association, 1974). This edition of the address, which adapts the original for gender inclusivity, is from http://onlineministries.creighton.edu/CollaborativeMinistry/men-for-others.html.

4. Pedro Arrupe, "Final Address of Father General to the Congregation of Procurators," in *The Spiritual Legacy of Pedro Arrupe, s.j.* (Rome: Jesuit Curia, 1985), 38.

5. From Pedro Arrupe, *Challenge to Religious Life Today,* ed. Jerome Aixala (St. Louis, MO: Institute of Jesuit Sources, 1979), 117–18.

6. From Pedro Arrupe, *Justice with Faith Today* (St. Louis, MO: Institute of Jesuit Sources, 1980), 103.

7. Unpublished Saying Attributed to Pedro Arrupe. Several Jesuit scholars have attempted to locate the original source of this quotation, including John Padberg, s.j., the director of the Institute of Jesuit Sources and Vincent O'Keefe, s.j., former general counselor under Pedro Arrupe. They have not been able to locate it, but have found significant evidence to suggest that the quotation is authentically from Arrupe. In a phone interview Fr. O'Keefe stated that he believed that the quotation came in answer to a question at a workshop that Fr. Arrupe was giving to a congregation of religious women, probably in the late 1970s.

8. From *Recollections and Reflections of Pedro Arrupe, s.j.*, (Wilmington, DE: Michael Glazier, 1986), 173.

George Ganss (1905–2000)

1. Joseph de Guibert, *The Jesuits: Their Spiritual Doctrine and Practice*, ed. George E. Ganss, trans. William J. Young (St. Louis, MO: Institute of Jesuit Sources, 1964), 537–38.

2. At that time the only important work of the early Jesuits in English was the text of the *Spiritual Exercises*, a book Ganss himself subsequently retranslated with substantial scholarly notes and an extensive introduction. Interestingly, Jesuits from India (where European languages other than English were also not commonly spoken) originally provided the greatest support for the importance of translations to the project of renewal. We are indebted to Fr. John Padberg, S.J., for his assistance with biographical material on Ganss.

3. This is the official and full "title" St. Ignatius gave to the book commonly referred to as the *Spiritual Exercises*.

4. George E. Ganss, "Endnotes on the Exercises," in *The Spiritual Exercises of Saint Ignatius*, trans. George E. Ganss (St. Louis, MO: The Institute of Jesuit Sources, 1992), 146–47.

5. From George E. Ganss, "Authentic Spiritual Exercises of St. Ignatius: A Brief History of Their Practice and Terminology," *Studies in the Spirituality of Jesuits* 1, no. 2 (St. Louis, MO: American Assistancy Seminar on Jesuit Spirituality, 1969), 11–12.

Josée Gsell (1925–1999) and Christian Life Communities

1. *The Spiritual Writings of Pierre Favre: The* Memoriale *and Selected Letters and Instructions*, ed. and trans. E. Murphy et al. (St. Louis, MO: Institute of Jesuit Sources, 1996), 39 and n. 86. See also John W. O'Malley, *The First Jesuits* (Cambridge, MA: Harvard University Press, 1993), 192–99. Both O'Malley and Murphy point to additional sources.

2. The primary languages of the world federation of sodalities were English, Spanish, and French. In the English language the world movement is called Christian Life Community (CLC), but in the Spanish and French the movement is called Communidad de Vida Christiana (CVX) and Communauté de Vie Chrétienne (CVX), respectively. The world logo and name thus combine both acronyms: CLC/CVX. Since this volume is addressed to an English-speaking audience, we refer to the Worldwide Christian Life Community by the abbreviated acronym CLC. We are indebted to the French CVX and the World Office of CLC/CVX for their assistance with biographical material on Josée Gsell.

3. GC 35, Decree 2, Collaboration at the Heart of Mission, 28.

4. Address of Fr. Adolfo Nicolás to the World Assembly of Christian Life Communities, August 17, 2008, Fatima, Portugal; accessed from http://www.cvx-clc .net/l-en/documents/nicolas_fatima08_en.pdf; December 21, 2008.

5. A dynamic youth program developed on the model of the JOC (Young Christian Workers) but for rural young adults. This Catholic action movement challenged lay Catholics to take seriously their baptismal responsibility to spread the Gospel in the world of work and ordinary secular culture. It was regarded with some suspicion and fear by some European bishops right up to the Second Vatican Council where its basic tenants were embedded in the Constitutions voted by the council and promulgated by Pope Paul VI.

6. This phrase was frequently applied to the Dominican and Jesuit theologians of Catholic renewal in France in the decade of 1944–1954. The energy of this movement was sharply curtailed by a conservative backlash from Rome in 1954.

7. The "Nineteenth Annotation" is a way of making the Exercises recommended by St. Ignatius for persons who cannot leave home or work for an extended period of time. It provides for undertaking the whole process of prayer, penance, and discernment, while remaining within one's ordinary daily life, over thirty or more weeks instead of an enclosed thirty-day retreat.

8. Christian Life Community–USA, *General Principles*, 8; accessed from http:// www.clc-usa.org/gpcharism.htm; December 21, 2008.

9. From Josée Gsell, *En Chemin Avec Marie*, trans. Eileen Burke-Sullivan, *Progressio* 11 (Rome: Christian Life Community World Center, April 1978): 39–42.

10. From *Louis Paulussen, s.j., Faithful Servant of Grace, Progressio* 37 (Rome: Christian Life Community World Center, April 1991): 28–31.

Afterword

1. Letter of Fr. Joseph Daoust, s.j., delegate at large from the Detroit Province (February 8, 2008).

2. Adolfo Nicholás, "Homily of the New Father General at the Mass of Thanksgiving" (January 21, 2008), Creighton University Online Ministries, http://www .creighton.edu/CollaborativeMinistry/GC35/CG35_2008-01-20%20Homily_eng .pdf.